"You're either well-lit with a goal of turning up your illumination and flame, or you're burned out. This book teaches you how to get lit, stay lit, and light others while feeling good all the time."

Mark Victor Hansen
Co-author, New York Times #1 Best-selling
CHICKEN SOUP FOR THE SOUL series

"This uplifting book gives you a 'flight plan' to soar with the eagles toward the realization of your full potential."

Brian Tracy
Business expert,
Author, *THE PSYCHOLOGY OF ACHIEVEMENT*

"Everyone should read GET FIRED UP WITHOUT BURNING OUT! It's loaded with unforgettable stories and solutions that work now."

Dottie Walters
World-class speaker, author, publisher

"As you read this book, you'll be encouraged, moved and inspired. You'll learn that anything is possible!"

Madeline Stone
Platinum-selling, award-winning songwriter

"GET FIRED UP WITHOUT BURNING OUT! is filled with answers for keeping life's passion alive. I recommend reading it to rekindle your flame."

Wally Amos
Author, *WATERMELON MAGIC: SEEDS OF WISDOM*
Founder, "FAMOUS AMOS" Cookies

GET FIRED UP
WITHOUT BURNING OUT™

CAROL GRACE ANDERSON, M.A.

Rock Hill Publishing
Nashville

Rock Hill Publishing
PO Box 148258
Nashville, TN 37214-8258

Phone: 615-885-9424
Toll-free: 877-446-9364
Fax: 615-885-2466
E-mail: RockHillBooks@aol.com

www.GetFiredUp.com

ISBN: 0-9660276-0-4
Third Edition
Printed in the USA
Sixth Printing

To

Mary Beth Anderson

With your Morning Glory heart, angel wings,
and signs in the sky ...
fly high!

CONTENTS

ACKNOWLEDGMENTS

To all those who help me keep fired up without burning out ...

Thanks for your support of every sort. I can't do it without you. Specifically, my wild, wonderful family: Jim, Lois, Lynn, Jerry, Jimmy, Jacqueline, J.J., Rory, Vince, and Nate the Great; my SPD (hossman); the Heavenly folks; Roy ... special thanks to a special friend ... you're part of the family; my dear, true friends; the Birthday Club; Al; and the pro's ... Jennie, Kittie, and Lynn.

INTRODUCTION

GET FIRED UP ... WITHOUT BURNING OUT! is a road map to discovering how great your life can be.

Do you know that you have a right to be happy every day? What's holding *you* back from living to the fullest? This book will give you the specifics that can change your life forever if you follow the simple suggestions. The steps don't have to be complicated or difficult ... they just have to be done.

Too busy? Is your life missing that special spark? Has your job become a drag? Are you missing out on all the passion and fun that you deserve? Look inside these pages to see how you can easily turn it all around. Read it over and over for reminders.

This book spells out how to take action *right now* to improve your attitude and relationships, enjoy your job, take responsibility, find balance, and be happier and more successful than ever!

Life is loaded with challenges. They can pull you down *or* you can grab those challenges for new strength, wisdom and empowerment.

You deserve a fired up, fantastic life! Make that choice. This book shows you the way. Enjoy the ride.

CHAPTER ONE

YOU GOTTA GET GOIN'

"You gotta get goin'
You gotta keep flowin'
You gotta keep movin' on
You gotta be knowin'
You gotta keep growin'
You gotta keep movin on

There's so much that you can do
All you gotta do is try
And keep believing in yourself
Keep shooting for the sky."

Carol Grace Anderson/Al McCree

It had two wheels. It was 18 feet long. It had one hitch ... to hook it up to the back of the car. It was our family home for years.

Our trailer (not much longer than a van) had one little bed that my older sister and I shared. Mom and Dad are tall, but willingly slept on a love seat that opened up to one short twin-size bed.

There was *almost* a kitchen. A tiny sink, small fold-down table and Coleman-type stove were the center of meals and all other fun stuff.

There was no bathroom. A little portable deal in the closet did the trick.

There WAS hope.

There was no air conditioner; when the summer sun would beat down on that dark gray aluminum, the inside thermostat would get stuck trying to edge past 105°.

There was no telephone. No TV.

There WAS love.

Our home on wheels was parked *very* close to others at a trailer park in New Jersey. We had rows and rows of company. Mostly circus performers who worked the Big Top in nearby New York City. A highly interesting bunch! More on them later.

A block or two down the road, there were public restrooms and showers. Also two wash machines (no dryers) and a public telephone.

We were often on financial and emotional edges. The pressure in that little space was intense. Dad's ministry paid him $25 a week and Mom taught some piano lessons. Sometimes we barely got by. But I learned something vital about getting fired up without burning out. My folks modeled it ...

You gotta have hope. And love. (And we *did* have a radio).

Until about the first grade, I thought everyone lived on wheels. And I figured the whole universe consisted of trailers, a few buildings, a school, a circus, and a church. Period.

Maybe that's why I've chosen a profession loaded with travel and new experiences. I'm still blown away by the vast tapestry of the world. It's as big as the possibilities.

From that tiny trailer, I never had a clue that I'd perform in Russia, earn a Master's degree from N.Y.U., land a role in a Paramount film, sing with Roy Clark, fly with the Blue Angels, meet Gregory Peck, perform on THE TONIGHT SHOW, have over 25 of my songs recorded, give motivational speeches to organizations across the country, write a book, or anything else. But I always had big dreams.

You've had your own challenges. Life is full of them. This book is about becoming the *champion of your challenges.* Restoring your hope. Becoming fully alive to the greatness that you are!

Because YOU are the most valuable, unique, powerful, wonderful asset you've got. And YOU CAN GET FIRED UP WITHOUT BURNING OUT! In fact, you can enjoy greater success, happiness, security, and balance than you ever thought possible.

Before you reach any destination, you have to start somewhere. You can start right here. Right now.

Experts say that 90% of all the energy used in a rocket mission is used during take-off! Once it gets rolling ... it gets easier. Moving on its own momentum.

Isn't this a lot like we are? Once we decide what we want to do, we've just got to get started. You gotta get goin'.

My Grandma Griscom used to say, "Well begun is half done." The longer I live, the more truth and value I find in that statement. Launching this book was really a matter of getting started.

DECIDE

Deciding that I needed to share this important and exciting information was the first step. Before we go anywhere, we have to make a *decision* to move ahead. You're deciding to read this book.

My Uncle Eddie decided that there should be an automatic donut machine on the market. (Hey, whatever floats your boat.) He had never seen one, so he created one.

After *many* trials and errors over several years, his invention is now all over the *world*. The machine makes mini-donuts, "Little Orbits", while you watch. They're really delicious, too. You've probably seen them at malls, fairs, conventions or sporting events.

Uncle Eddie has put thousands of people into business for themselves by selling entrepreneurs the machine and all the supplies. Everybody wins.

After I decided that I wanted to share this information that *works*, then I decided to begin by writing it down ... to bite the bullet and just get going.

> ### *"There's nothing like the momentum of taking action."*
>
> ### *CGA*

First, decide *where* you want to go. What are your goals? What are you putting off? What areas of your life need a jump-start? If your answer is "all of them," don't panic. There's hope. Keep reading.

Everyone needs a plan. Imagine driving to the airport, parking, arriving at the boarding gate on time, boarding the plane, and hearing the pilot say, "I have no earthly idea of our destination this morning, but welcome aboard." Unless you intended to go on one of those mystery trips, this would sound pretty strange, wouldn't it? You want the pilot to have a plan. You trust it matches your plan.

You have to decide your goals. And only *you* can do that. Of course, the consideration of your responsibilities is weaved into that decision. It's that "grown-up" thing we all know and love.

GOING FOR THE GOALS

I've heard my colleagues say, "If you fail to plan, you plan to fail." It makes a lot of sense. Getting a plan is key.

Oprah Winfrey had a plan. She set a goal of running a 26-mile marathon. Whew. She did it! How? By getting started. By working at it every day. Then ... by putting one foot in front of the other for 26 miles. She felt great crossing the finish line.

"Destiny is not a matter of chance;
it is a matter of choice.
It is not a thing to be waited for;
it is a thing to be achieved."

William Jennings Bryan

What are some of your goals?

Learning to ski?	Creating more family time?
Writing an article?	Starting a business?
Raising your income?	Learning to fly?
Taking a class?	Moving up to manager?
Climbing Mt. Everest?	Becoming a doctor?
Using your creativity?	Playing an instrument?
Writing a song?	Volunteering more?

My friend Jeannie is very creative and has a knack for adding a small touch that brings big results. About twelve years ago, she added a beautiful bow to a small teddy bear. It looked great. She started adding other things ... hats, outfits, pins, etc. Her friends and neighbors wanted to buy them ... for themselves and as gifts.

Jeannie now had a goal; she wanted to make these teddy bears available to everyone who wanted one. She had to figure out how to work that out. She took one step at a time. She got going.

Jeannie and her husband Bobby opened a small teddy bear store to keep up with the demand. They now have a larger store, a full staff, a huge inventory and ship bears all over the world. The store is THE BOBBY BARE TRAP, located in Nashville, TN.

What's your plan? What can make your life richer, fuller, more balanced?

---

*"Put guts into
your goals."*

CGA

SOME STARTING STEPS

Step 1: **ERASE EXCUSES.** Stop listening to negative people or your own negative inner voice making tired old excuses. You've heard them ... here are some samples:

"I'll start later."
"When I have more money, I'll do something."
"I don't have what it takes to do it right."
"I'm not that lucky."
"I'll wait 'til the kids move out."
"I was never a go-getter."
"That's for someone younger."
"One person can't make a difference."
"In the spring, I can get going."
"Aw, it's not worth the trouble."
"If I had more time, I'd do it."

Step 2: **WRITE DOWN GOALS.** Something happens when you commit your goals to paper. It's as though you're telling the world: "I'm serious about this."

Comedian Jim Carrey, when he was broke, trying to get going as a stand-up comic in L.A., wrote himself a check. The amount? Ten million dollars! He kept it in his wallet ... year after year. He now receives more than that for each movie he makes.

Step 3: **CATEGORIZE GOALS.** Goals are helpful in all areas of our lives:

Work - This is important. Work is valuable to our sense of well-being ... financially and emotionally. We're contributing something. But work *ain't* everything.

Family - In the big picture, we can clearly see the strength and power of the family unit ... our family of friends included. Sociologists have been telling us that for years, but it seems to hit home now more than ever.

Health - If we're not feeling up to par, or are down-right sick, everything sure changes in a hurry. My brother Jim was part of a news crew that covered the last big birthday bash Malcolm Forbes threw before he died. Forbes flew Liz Taylor, William F. Buckley, Barbara Walters and hundreds of others to Morocco to celebrate in style. Wouldn't he have traded his millions for good health?

Spirituality - What is our purpose, anyway? Why are we here? This has been one of the most discussed, analyzed topics throughout history. And there is a renewed interest with the spiritual side of life. It's important. Check out the best-seller lists. We're hungry for more information. We want more answers. And we want the right answers in this department.

Step 4: **BE SPECIFIC:** What are your immediate goals in each category? Example, your goals for today? How about your mid-range goals? Such as next week ... next month. What are your long-range goals? Where do you see yourself next year? In five years? What do you want your life to look like in ten years?

Here's a sample: Instead of saying, "I'd like to spend more time with my family." Say, "I'm devoting Saturday afternoon to a fun outing with the family." Get into the habit of scheduling more time together. Don't cancel.

Instead of saying, "I need to save money," say, "I will put 10% of my monthly income in a savings account starting this month."

Instead of saying, "I want to learn to play golf some day," say, "I'm going to call right now and schedule a lesson for this week."

Step 5: **REVIEW AND RE-DO:** Go over your goal list regularly. Check off all those things you completed ... notice them ... celebrate them! Evaluate the ones that are left. Add new ones. Keep going and growing.

Those are FIVE STEPS that can get you started today.

Here are some spaces to get you rolling:

★ Two of my goals for today are:

1. _____

2. _____

★ Two goals for this week are:

1. _____

2. _____

★ Two goals for this month are:

1. _____

2. _____

Stay in close touch with your goals. They're your plan of action. If you start with short-term goals and stick to them, you'll be getting into the habit of goal-reaching. A wonderful feeling.

For example, if one of your mid-range goals is to feel more energized and get healthier, you could start right now by setting up a physical exam with your doctor. You could add a walk into your schedule today. That's do-able. You could start substituting a piece of fruit for dessert, start drinking more water, cutting down on fats, increasing vegetable intake. You know what it takes. You've just gotta get goin'.

"Small steps
can bring
huge results."

CGA

SO, WHY AREN'T WE DOIN' IT?

You've met someone who is loaded with potential but can't seem to get going, right?

I used to date a guy who was brilliant. His goal was to be a college professor. He would have been a great addition to any faculty. One problem; he quit college with only one course to go. And it was not nearly as challenging a subject as some he had sailed through easily. Why?

A neighbor was up for a huge promotion. Her income and responsibilites would increase. She had looked forward to the challenge for a long time. It was finally coming through. But she handed in her resignation two days before the promotion became effective. Why?

FEAR

This is *not* responsible concern we're talking about. We all need some of that. That's why we stay out of the path of an oncoming train. That's why we use seatbelts ... and have smoke alarms. That's why we tend to crying babies who need our help.

But FEAR keeps us from getting fired up. It can paralyze us.

"Fear is a four-letter word."

CGA

WHAT ARE WE AFRAID OF?

1. FEAR OF THE UNKNOWN: If we're not too sure of the outcome, we might have such fear that we'd rather not even try.

Recently I was invited to speak to some County Executives. They needed a motivational message. Part of the deal was that they were all going white-water rafting after the meeting and invited me to go along.

I'm not much into water sports, but on a whim, I agreed. As soon as I had committed, and hung up the phone, I was terrified. This was the Ocoee River in Tennessee ... where they held the Olympic white-water events!

What if I fell out of the raft and went crashing into the rocks?

What if we all drowned and were never heard from again?

What if the water's too cold? What if ... what if ...

I felt my fear, but did it anyway. What a thrill! I'm so glad I didn't wimp out. That was an unforgettable experience. But one I came *that* close to missing.

Is fear of the unknown holding you back from some great opportunities?

2. FEAR OF FAILURE: If we're not strong in the self-esteem department, this fear can really hold us back. It's the feeling that "if I don't do it right, what will they think of me?" "What if I ask her/him out and he/she says no?" "What if I take guitar lessons and I'm not that good?" "If my golf ball lands in the sand trap ... what'll they say?"

Who are *they* anyway? They haven't done us any good so far.

It's much easier to *not* take action. To let our fear of failure win out and hold ourselves back from learning and growing. Imagine where we'd be if we let this kind of thinking take charge. We'd never have learned to walk, run, ride a bike, drive, type ... you name it. The list goes on.

Fear of failure keeps us from lots of life's wonderful experiences.

3. FEAR OF SUCCESS: Yup, that's right. Success. Some people are so afraid of it, they'd rather not go for it.

Why? Some feel that they'd lose their friends or family if they're too successful. "How would I look making more money than my parents?" "Wouldn't my friends think I had an attitude driving up in a new car?"

Or ... "What if I became successful and lost it all?" "Wouldn't they think I was a jerk?" "I don't have what it takes for success anyway." "If I finish that course, I'll be a college graduate. They'll expect more from me than I can deliver."

WHAT TO DO?

ACKNOWLEDGE THE FEAR: This disarms it to a degree. I've heard some professional speakers say at the beginning of a program, "I want you all to know that I'm a little nervous." Then they often go on to give a smooth, relaxed speech.

It's okay to admit feeling fear. We *all* have some. You're not alone by any means.

TAKE ACTION: That's the second step in dealing with fear. Confront it. You have to go through the fear, not around it, to get to the other side of it. This is not about taking dangerous risks, becoming a dare-devil. We'll leave that to Evel Knievel.

It's about taking reasonable action on what we're fearing. For example; let's say you've been due a raise and haven't heard anything. It's time to go through the proper channels and ask about it. You feel uncomfortable at the thought of it. What would help you to take action?

Practice it on your own. Do some role-playing with a friend or family member. You'll be more prepared to take action. You'll have an idea of what it will feel like.

Maybe a friend asks you to join yet another committee. You're overbooked as it is. You hate to say no to a friend ... but you're swamped. Practice saying, "No, I can't now, but I hope you find just the right person." No big song and dance is necessary. More about that later.

Let's say you've been wanting to quit smoking. Maybe you've been putting it off for fear of failure. Taking action today is how to begin that process. And it is a process; not just an event. It's that "one day at a time" message. It IS possible or there would not be millions who have become smoke-free. (I'm one of 'em.)

FROM FEAR TO FANTASTIC

My Dad is a minister and youth worker to teens in the inner city. Some years ago, he noticed a tall (6'9"), gangly guy who slouched when he walked ... embarrassed at being much taller than the other guys. Afraid he didn't fit in.

Dad befriended him and tried to encourage him to overcome his shyness. "Why aren't you on the basketball team? You've got it made! Wake up and smell the coffee," Dad told him.

"Ah, I'm no good at basketball," he mumbled.

"They really need you on the high school team," Dad kept insisting. Then he called the coach: "How can you let this guy slip through your hands?"

Slowly this tall, shy guy started shooting some hoops on his own. He got the hang of it pretty quickly and actually had fun doing it. His height gave him an edge in dunking the ball and soon his friends were asking him for some pointers.

Ed Pinckney became a valuable member of the high school team there in the Bronx. About three years later, my Dad was surfing the TV channels and, by chance, stopped on a college basketball game. Not a real TV sports fan, he was ready to move on when he heard the announcer say, "Villanova's Ed Pinckney will go to the free-throw line as the team smothers Georgetown!"

Yes, Ed had gone on to college at Villanova, where he became the Most Valuable Player. Ed turned pro and played for the Boston Celtics, then the Philadelphia 76ers.

He overcame his fear and got some goals. Then he took action! That action brought him great success. Ed was fired up!

"You don't go from ZERO to HERO without working at it."

CGA

LADIES AND GENTLEMEN ... START YOUR ENGINES

How do you get going? Get some goals! Ask yourself, "What results do I want?" Decide what's top priority and begin to take action. If the task seems too overwhelming, break it down into sections. Take one step at a time. Start NOW.

Let's say you want to change jobs. That's your goal. Start now by doing some research on what job you'd like to go to. Ask yourself, "If I had many options, which would I choose? What are some things I really like to do?" Make a detailed list. Include everything ... don't hold back.

Then look at all the pros and cons of each possibility. Learn about it. Talk to people in different types of work. Network all you can. Keep your résumé updated and looking professional. Visit some companies or job sites. Get a feel for the environment. Start.

Maybe your dream has been to take a trip to another part of the country. Follow the same procedure to zone in on where you'd like to go, how you want to get there, what time of year, where you'd stay, what your budget is, etc.

When you've got your goals clearly in your mind, map out a plan to get you there. Builders need a detailed blueprint to follow to get that building completed. We also need a map; a blueprint; a plan.

Goals are dreams that require *action*. They're what we're aiming for. The goal post is the winning line. Reaching the mark means successfully reaching our goals ... whatever they are.

You've got a lot to offer. Stop waiting around. You gotta get goin'!

REVIEW

YOU GOTTA GET GOIN' ... take the first steps ... to get fired up!

Here's how:

DECIDE what you want to do to improve your life.

Go for your GOALS

> 1. Erase Excuses
> 2. Write Down Goals
> 3. Categorize Them
> 4. Be Specific
> 5. Review and Re-do

Let go of FEAR

> 1. Acknowledge It
> 2. Take Action

CHAPTER TWO

JUST A REACH AWAY

"Just a reach away there's something better
Something that you never thought about.
You know the sun will always follow stormy weather.
You might be feeling down, but you ain't out."

Anderson/McCree

Each one of us is unique. Think about that. Of the billions of people who have lived on this earth ... no two are exactly alike. Incredible.

Because we're all different, we each have unique talents and strengths ... something special to offer. Yet we're not living up to our potential, (only about 5% of the population is doing that ... more on this later), but we *can* work toward it. It's just a reach away.

It may not be easy. Life is not always a pleasant stroll in the park. It is tough. There are peaks and valleys, turns and straight roads, good times and bad. But, there's hope! Yes, for you.

When I take off on a flight during rainy weather, I'm always amazed at the short time it takes before we're above the clouds and the sun is shining big as life. It was always there ... we just couldn't see it. It was just a reach away.

Sociologists have come up with an interesting finding; one important factor in longevity is resilience. The ability to bounce back after grieving a loss of any kind ... and moving forward.

We've got to get our goals lined up and *know* that we can move forward. Know that it's just a reach away.

"You've got to do what
you have to do ...
to do what you want to do."

Dolly Parton

NOT COLLEGE MATERIAL

When I was a senior in high school, I dropped by the Guidance Office to ask about college applications. Mr. Shaw, the counselor there, said, "Carol, you don't plan on going to college, do you? You're *not* college material. Look at your grades!"

That hit me like a ton of bricks. Not college material? But I wanted to be a teacher or a social worker like my older sister, Lynn. You need a degree for those choices.

I had to admit to myself that I had been majoring in majorettes. I loved being part of the twirling team. We even twirled fire. Wow, talk about getting fired up. That was much more interesting than history or geometry, let's face it.

Anyway, I was admitted to a small college in upstate New York for the summer session ... with the stipulation that I get at least a "C" in two courses. I got a "D" and an "F". Whoops.

My parents frantically tried to help me. They found another small college that would take anyone with a pulse. I was in! But after hanging in for three semesters, I flunked out. A third try, at another college, brought the same dismal result.

I was now pretty sure Mr. Shaw was right. On the other hand, I knew, in my heart, that I *could* do whatever it took to get a degree. It was just a reach away.

Setting my mind to it was the key. I started taking one
course at a time at a local Community College. I earned my
Associate degree there ... graduating with honors. A great
feeling! From there I went on to receive a B.A. in
Psychology from Bloomfield College and an M.A. in
Counselor Education from New York University. (The same
degree as Mr. Shaw.)

It sure didn't take a genius IQ , but it took "stick-to-it-
ive-ness." Is that a word? Maybe I just made it up. It works.

Think of all you've accomplished when you've set your
mind to it.

---

*"Reaching high ...
keeps you on
your toes!"*

Unknown

REACH FOR YOUR OLYMPIC-SIZE DREAMS

Faster. Higher. Stronger. They weren't kidding around! I
get caught up in the Olympic spirit as many of you do. How
do they DO that? Just to qualify is a huge deal.

We can learn some lessons from this lively, top-shape, top-notch bunch of winners. In the interviews and in-depth background stories of these incredible athletes, I get an idea of what it takes for them to realize their Olympic-size dreams. What they teach us, we can apply to *our* goals.

I've simplified it into three R's:

1. REACH - The dictionary defines this as, "to stretch forth; to extend." That's precisely what we've got to do to move forward and grow. Learning is really reaching ... stretching our knowledge and experience.

The late Wilma Rudolph was a great Olympian and role model. She was the 20th of 22 kids in her family. Instead of moping around and complaining that she had to wear hand-me-downs and share parental love with so many siblings, she had a great spark for life.

She suffered from childhood polio at age four, resulting in a struggle to walk. She was fitted with a leg brace. She felt clumsy and awkward but she never complained ... instead she *reached*. She learned to walk and run. Run fast. To gold medals!

In the 1996 Olympics, runner Michael Johnson reached ... wearing shiny, gold, running shoes. He stretched his old records and reached new heights in the history books.

A decade earlier, Mary Lou Retton reached for perfect 10's in gymnastistics ... and got 'em.

HE SAW THE LIGHT

When I think of reaching, I remember Thomas Edison. During an interview, motivator Napoleon Hill asked, "Mr. Edison, what have you got to say about the fact that you failed thousands of times in your attempts to create a light bulb?"

Edison answered, "I beg your pardon. I've never failed even once. I've had thousands of learning experiments that didn't work. I had to run through enough experiences to find a way that it *did* work."

Thomas Edison could have easily given up after 999 tries at creating the light bulb. But he kept moving forward ... slowly but patiently. Learning every step of the way. Knowing the answer was just a reach away. Can you count the times you've enjoyed his invention already today?

Make a commitment to yourself to reach beyond where you are. Reach toward greater heights in all areas of your life; your work, your family life, your health, and spiritual side. You, your job, and your loved ones will all benefit. Good spreads around.

2. RISK - You've probably had it up to here with the "comfort zone" philosophies ... going beyond the familiar. But, you know what? We *do* have to go outside of our "comfort zone" to go for our goals and grow. Risk is often a scary proposition ... but that's where the good stuff starts. Taking risks. Reasonable risks.

> ## *"Smooth seas do not make great sailors."*
>
> **Sign in front of a church**

I want to distinguish between reasonable and unreasonable risks. For seven years, I was a singer in the Roy Clark show, as I mentioned. Yes, the guitar and entertaining legend Roy Clark. And yes, he's as nice as he seems. Really. What a fantastic experience that was!

The first few years, most of the shows we did were in Las Vegas, Reno, and Lake Tahoe (breathtaking!)

Growing up in a tiny trailer park, then the hamlet of Godeffroy, New York ... between Huguenot and Cuddebackville ... then living in New York City a short time ... then Nashville ... I had never been *near* a casino. Gambling was only legal in Nevada at the time.

Now, in the early 1980s, I was living in casino hotels for weeks at a time as a singer in the show. Quite a colorful experience. The food was always wonderful as I recall ... attracting customers to play the slot machines, blackjack, craps and roulette before and after meals. Sometimes instead of meals.

IT'S A GAMBLE

There's an element of excitement in a casino. Machines clanging, dropping heavy coins into metal trays, bells ringing, patrons squealing in delight ... and NO CLOCKS. Cocktail waitresses are serving free drinks and everyone is having a blast.

Or so it seems. What you DON'T see is the sweet older woman in the corner, hands black from coin metal, her face lined with sadness. It's 3:00 a.m. and she's risking her last few dollars for the month, hoping for a lucky break. One more pull on the slot machine.

What you DON'T see is the well-dressed young man in his late 20's calling desperately to his family in Persia. Tears streaming down his face. He had lost several thousand dollars playing high-stake blackjack. In trying to change his luck and win it back, he lost thousands more. With the magic of credit cards, he used up his family's entire life savings. He couldn't afford an airline ticket home.

I met these people. It was sad. They thought happiness and success were just a reach away on the slot machine. They're examples of *unreasonable* risk. Casinos make huge profits from patrons taking these risks. Experts say, "Gamble only what you can afford to lose." The odds always favor the casino. Remember that, if you're going to play.

On to *reasonable* risk. We started as babies, moving from crawling to standing to walking. That took risk. Not to mention scraped knees and bumped foreheads. If we didn't risk it, we'd still be crawling. Stuck in our old but familiar ways.

Because we took those risks, we could learn to walk, run, skip, jump, dance, ski, skate. They became a natural part of our lives.

As adults we still have to take risks to move ahead. The Olympic athletes go to the edge. They have to find balance between breaking records and breaking bones. Not only do they REACH ... but they RISK.

3. RESOLVE - Determination! We've all made New Year's resolutions. We promised ... were determined ... to improve our lives once and for all. But if we didn't "resolve" every single day, backed up with action, we saw no results. Agree?

To resolve takes heart and commitment. The Olympians work hard, long, lonely hours. There's no glamour, no press, no glory in their preparation. Their passion gives them resolve, determination, to hang in and hang on. We need *that* kind of resolve.

Prisoners of war exist in the worst of circumstances. They could be done in at the drop of a hat if it weren't for their resolve. Their determination is so powerful, it gets them through. It saves them.

If we mean business about reaching our goals, we've got to break through that wall of self-doubt. We need to take a deep breath and keep pressing on ... even when it would be much easier to throw in the towel. Easier to lower our standards. Easier to hope we'll get lucky and find success and happiness on a silver platter. That doesn't happen here in the real world.

> *"Throwing in the towel only leads to a bigger pile of laundry."*
>
> *CGA*

It's not always easy to reach, risk, and resolve. It takes hard work. It requires keeping your eye on the prize. It means keeping passionate about your goals. Keeping focused.

Enjoying the results are worth any challenges on the journey. And of course, we can *always* count on those challenges showing up.

> *"Courage is the price*
> *that life exacts*
> *for granting peace.*
> *The soul that knows it not,*
> *knows no release*
> *From little things;*
> *Knows not the livid*
> *loneliness of fear,*
> *Nor mountain heights*
> *where bitter joy can hear*
> *The sound of wings."*
>
> *Amelia Earhart*

TURN STRUGGLE INTO STRENGTH

My great dog, Callie, loves to walk ... anywhere, anytime, any weather. It's fun to walk with her and share some of her wonder at everything. I've learned a lot. How to be more fully observant is one major thing.

Last spring I noticed on one of our paths a green leaf growing right out of an old, hard, railroad tie. There it was all by itself. Surviving in the aged wood.

This spring, I looked at the same old railroad tie and there was a beautiful, delicate pink flower ... flourishing. What a standout!

What a metaphor for life. In the most difficult and unlikely of circumstances, we can bloom. We can grow. It may be a struggle but it is POSSIBLE.

BREAK OUT OF YOUR PRISON

The first fulltime job I landed after college was teaching a Psychology course to adults. My students had a perfect attendance record and filled every seat in the classroom. Every teacher's dream.

Did I mention that all the students were men?

Did I mention that this was a prison for male heroin addicts who were doing time for drug-related felonies?

Quite a challenge. Working behind bars was a very new experience. I may have learned a lot more than they did.

The men ranged in age from 18 to 72. All of them had choices in the education department. They could learn a trade (barbering, welding, or woodworking) and take some academic courses ... from high school to college level.

These inmates were full of potential. Some were great poets, artists, musicians. The challenge they faced on leaving the facility was to change their entire lives when they "got back on the street." Convicted felons have a difficult time getting legitimate work. It's not easy to change your environment and start new friendships and relationships as an adult with a prison record. But IT IS POSSIBLE.

"BIG BAD JOHN"

I'll never forget one very capable student in my class. John loved to take exams ... maybe it was the challenge to get a high score. He was a treasure. Tattooed on his arm was "Big Bad John" but under his tough exterior was a sweet, kind person.

After taking my courses for two years, John's release date came up. Our last class together was over.

"You've got what it takes to make it out there," I said. "You may have a tough-as-nails exterior, but you've got a heart of gold. You're a *good* person."

John had been looking down. When he raised his head, a big, single tear slowly rolled down his face. "No one ever told me that before," John whispered ... his voice cracking. "Thank you."

I never saw John again. Whatever he made of his life was just a reach away. I've heard long-distance runners talk about "going through the wall." They kept going no matter how hard the road became. That's what separates the real winners in life. They *know* it's just a reach away.

HOW TO FALL IN LOVE WITH YOUR JOB

Success at anything is just a reach away ... even falling in love with your job. Using the same 3-R formula discussed earlier in this chapter, it becomes easy to do.

REACH: Imagine how fun work could be if we made it more of a game. A fun challenge. It can be done!

Think of brand new ways to do your job. Imagine that you own the company, the plant, the agency, the store, the whatever. Ask yourself how your job should be done if you were in charge of the whole thing ... and you wanted to expand and improve the company. *Reach* for new answers.

Do some research to find out more about your specific job, your company, your product, your service. Information is powerful. It'll help you know how you can improve.

Show up on the job with an upbeat, can-do attitude ... even if you have to *reach* for it. In the following chapters you'll find specifics to guarantee a great attitude.

Make it a point to *reach out* to others who could use some help, too. That creates a unified spirit at work. If it's not there, you could be the one to start it!

RISK: Begin by putting some of this new information into practice. It's a risk because it's new and you're not familiar with it yet. Your co-workers may be shaky with it, too. Take small steps. Get comfortable with it. Even minor changes take some getting used to.

Let's say you're in sales. Try a new approach. If you're accustomed to a soft-sell approach, experiment with a more direct, assertive style. Try several different things. Remember, for different results, we have to do something different.

Maybe you're an administrative assistant. What are some ways you could work more efficiently or even expand your responsibilities? That could be very helpful to you and management. It would also make the job more exciting.

If you're a teacher, think of fresh, new ways to present the same information. Experiment. It'll be more fun for you and the students.

Share what you're learning with the leadership. Make suggestions. Lots of improvements happened because someone like you reached and took risks to move forward. Managers, CEOs, and successful inventors followed those steps.

RESOLVE: You can fall in love with your job by making a commitment to it. One important way to get to that point is to write down on a sheet of paper ten things you *like* about your job. Yes, it's much more common to be aware of the negatives. Change that.

In these times of incredible and constant change, to HAVE a job is something to be thankful for. Notice even the small positives ... maybe your job is close to home; has good coffee; predictable hours; good benefits; some nice co-workers; is good exercise; is challenging, etc.

Think of some jobs that you know are much worse than yours by a long shot. That may help you appreciate what you have.

The more you love your job, the more the job will love you! You'll be a more valuable part of it all.

REACH, RISK, RESOLVE. You *can* get fired up about your job!

REVIEW

You can get fired up ... it's JUST A REACH AWAY

It's out there for you, you just have to do what it takes to get it. Even loving your job is just a reach away.

Here's my simple 3-R FORMULA:

1. REACH - The great thinkers, great athletes, great leaders, great inventors, great goal-getters ... they all have to reach toward greater heights. Do the same thing to fall in love with your job.

2. RISK - We have to move from comfort to challenge to grow. Learning to walk took risk and maybe a few skinned-up knees, but look at the great payoff. Take some risks to grow in your job and everything else.

3. RESOLVE - Make a commitment. Be determined. Don't give up even when the going gets rough. Reaching your goals means hanging in there.

CHAPTER THREE

NOW

"Yesterday is gone forever
And it's never comin' back.
Tomorrow is out there somewhere
Way on down the track.
Take a look at the clock it will prove it
When it comes right down to it
All we really ever have is now."

Carol Grace Anderson

"Mommy, mommy, when are we gonna go bye-bye?"

"Shut up ... we ARE bye-bye!"

I was a young kid at Point Pleasant (New Jersey) beach with my family when we heard the woman on the blanket near us have that exact exchange with her little son. He'd had enough sand, wind, sun, and salt water for one day.

He wasn't enjoying the present moment any longer ...
to say the least.

My family and I have had lots of laughs over that.

It's easy to get caught up in what I call "future living."
That little kid on the beach hoping "bye bye" will be better.
It means holding out for some other time that isn't here yet.

Here are some examples that may sound familiar:

"Let's save the good plates just for special occasions."

"I better not wear my favorite outfit too often ... it'll
wear out too fast."

"When we retire, we can think about having some fun."

"You better save for a rainy day."

"I'll invite you over when the house is painted."

"Some day, I'll learn to dance."

"We can relax when we start our vacation."

There's one big problem with this "future-living;" we
miss NOW. I'm not referring to being responsible grownups and planning for a future. This is about living. And we
can *only* live NOW!

Think about it.

Some Tibetan Monks celebrate the importance of the "present" with an interesting art form ... sand painting. They spend days totally focused on creating beautiful works out of sand. The intricacy and difficulty takes a lot of patience and artistic skill.

When they have completed the work, and everything is in place, they blow air over the piece to disperse every grain of sand.

The whole value of the work was in creating it and seeing the finished product for a moment. They are celebrating NOW.

"Yesterday is history,
tomorrow is a mystery,
and today is a gift ...
that's why they
call it the present."

Unknown

THE PRESENT

"There's no time like the present." We've always heard that. Right? That's because it's TRUE. It really is all we've got.

The past is over, tomorrow's not here yet, so let's look at what's left. Now. Now is the time. This very moment matters.

Our culture is so geared toward racing into the future, it takes a conscious effort to be more mindful about living in the present.

You may know colleagues (not *you* of course), who spend beautiful vacation afternoons at the lake planning new marketing strategies. Others who would not be caught with their lap-tops down, their cell-phones within easy reach, their calculators crunching numbers.

Or, maybe you have friends who are always so busy doing *whatever*, they're never here ... in this moment. It seems like they're rushing through the day, even rushing through the night while they're sleeping. Trying to hurry that up, too!

I often found myself trying to capture great moments on video. On many occasions, I spent so much time focusing on camera angles, battery power, the lighting and framing, I missed the moment! There's nothing wrong with video cameras. They can create treasures. But let's not sacrifice the here-and-now for the future.

ENJOYING THE LEAN TIMES

A friend of mine is a very successful record producer. It was a long road to the top of the charts and listeners' hearts.

Years ago, I'd see him "pitching" his new rock act to major labels in New York. He'd set up showcases for industry people ... only to have a few pop in, see the empty place, and leave. He'd drop off new, expensive demos of the group. "Leave the tape and we'll get back with you," they'd tell him. They never did.

He tried to book the act in popular clubs all over the country. Club owners would tell him, "These guys won't draw flies. Nobody knows them."

The group and my friend never stopped believing and working at it. They were full of hope and humor, even when they were broke. Sometimes, they literally had three dollars between them.

The breakthrough came when a hit songwriter who liked their sound sent them a new song to record. They loved the song, borrowed some money and recorded it the next day.

My friend took the tape to all the labels who had turned him down. This time he got their attention ... and two substantial offers within the week.

The song was a #1 hit on the pop music charts and many more followed. Big bucks came pouring in to all of them.

Some years later I ran into my friend and asked him how he liked all that financial and artistic success.

"It's fine," he said, "but, truthfully, I had as much fun on the journey. It's not the money that makes you happy, it's enjoying life wherever you are now. We had a lot of laughs during those lean years ... it was fun. We were following our crazy dreams, barely scraping by. I wouldn't trade that for anything."

EXPERIENCE YOUR "PRESENT POWER"

Being mindful of the moment, the now, I call "Present Power." It takes practice and reminders to get there. The more often you experience it, the more natural it will become. We've ALL been there already. It's just a matter of bringing it back.

My niece Jacqueline and her husband Vince just had their first baby, Nathaniel. What a sweetie. He already has a definite, unique personality. Nathan reminds me how powerful this moment is ... he lives it to the max!

When we all were babies, we lived in the present. We reacted fully in the moment. We knew when we were happy, hungry, wet, sad, scared, cold, sick, entertained ... and we'd let those feelings be known. The moment was all that mattered.

There was no concern about the "good" dishes, the retirement package, the year-end sales records, or the rainy day.

As young kids we were still filled with that wonder of the moment; lost in a fairytale, a romp in a grassy field, Sesame Street, a tricycle, a goldfish, a doll, a coloring book, a truck.

---

*"**Now** is really*
the only time
we have."

CGA

Since we've been there before, and we're always really there, let's take a trip to NOW. For a moment, let's focus on the present. Here goes:

Put both feet on the floor and take a deep breath, breathing out slowly. Do it again. You're probably feeling a little more relaxed already. Notice how this book feels in your hands. Check out the texture and weight of it. Look closely at the letters on the page, see how they're arranged.

Take note of how you're sitting. Notice the feeling of your weight on the chair. Notice what your clothes feel like on you. Look at the texture and design.

How are you feeling? Good? Tired? Rested? Anxious? Relaxed? Comfortable?   Think of every feeling and sensation you can. Notice each one. Experience them. This is a moment of "Present Power."

MOSCOW AT MIDNIGHT

Here's a great example of being fully alive while we're here: In 1988, my sister Mary Beth and I went to Moscow and Leningrad (now St. Petersburg) on a Concert/ Friendship Tour. We were invited as part of the show and we even sang a song in Russian. Although, later some Russians wondered *what* language we were singing in!

Along with the band, an entire film crew came along. What a group! They brought cases of American snacks after hearing that the food in Russia was very, uh, different. (They were well-informed.)

We took off from JFK airport on a cold November evening, laughed with the band and crew all night and landed the next morning in Germany. After a scrumptious brunch at a nearby restaurant in Frankfurt, we took off for Moscow.

Arriving at around 9:00 p.m., Russia looked dark and mysterious. A dusting of snow added to the ambiance. We sailed through customs (in about three hours), loaded onto a bus, and made our way to the train station. We were greeted by our Russian host, Inna. She led us in a toast ... and to our compartments on the train.

By now, the snow was falling heavily. It was cozy. Mary Beth figured out how to put the table up in our little compartment as we rolled out of Moscow at midnight.

We saw a button on the wall, turned it, and heard beautiful classical music piped in. Neat! When we scraped a thin layer of ice off the window with a credit card, there was the countryside. Glimpses highlighted only by the snow in the dark. Or the warm glow from a fireplace in a small cottage near the tracks.

It was about 2:00 a.m. When we opened our compartment door to check out the footsteps in the hall, we met a uniformed man with a tea pot. He grunted a question to us in Russian. We smiled blankly. In a minute he returned with two glass cups of hot tea in fancy, silvery holders. Mmmmm.

Music, tea, snow, mystery. We'd been up now for two days. How could we go to sleep in such an enchanting setting?

Mary Beth taught me to cherish moments like that. A great gift.

MORE OF MARY BETH

In October of '95, I was learning more about living in the moment than I ever dreamed of. Mary Beth was in a valiant struggle with breast cancer. It had metastasized (spread) to her hip and spine.

Our entire family pitched in ... helping with trips to hospitals for chemo and radiation, finding special vitamin therapies, holding prayer services, cooking organic foods, anything we could think of to keep her around. She had always been in excellent health. This was foreign. Mary Beth was the most angelic person on earth. She *couldn't* leave.

The doctors couldn't get over her great attitude and mobility after they'd look at her x-rays. She was being driven by sheer will and determination. Living every moment to the fullest!

Just two months before her heavenly flight, Mary Beth went on a boat trip with our brother and several friends ... she sang and played guitar at a birthday party ... she went out to dinner followed by a stop at a blues club ... she created several beautiful water-color paintings ... she danced ... she completed her book of poetry (very inspirational) ... and finished a gorgeous colored-pencil drawing of a Mandala. Her philosophy of life in a circle rich with symbols.

We all had hope. But just a few weeks later she was hospitalized and the doctors said, "She doesn't have long. You'd better call the whole family in."

There was never a time in my life that I wanted to treasure every morsel of every moment any more than at that time. We cancelled everything and camped out (literally) at Vanderbilt University Medical Center.

The family came from New York, New Jersey, Boston, California and Nashville. We all had to savor these precious moments. Eating and sleeping took a backseat. Talking to Mary Beth ... holding her hand ... telling her how much we loved her ... praying ... singing to her ... that's all that mattered.

Three days later, we were all with her as she left this earth. An angel returning home. Surprisingly, it was a tranquil, powerful and triumphant moment ... mixed with undefinable grief and sadness.

I miss Mary Beth daily ... painfully at times. Other times with joyful memories ... grateful to have known her at all. We were very close and it's a huge loss. There's no way to minimize it.

On the plus side, I wanted to tell you about this because she taught us all a tremendous lesson. I want to share it with you. It's simply this:

Death is __not__ the worst tragedy.
To not be fully alive when we __are__
here is the worst tragedy.

A lesson lived by Mary Beth Anderson

THE PAST

Life is a series of moments strung together. Those moments we've spent already, are the past. They're over. History. But without the past, we wouldn't be here talking about this. It is important.

Since you and I are human, at least *most* of the time, join me in declaring it our "past imperfect." Hopefully, we were doing our best with what we knew at the time. We've come quite a long way, haven't we?

Time is a powerful teacher. Wouldn't it be amazing to do a few things over with the better tools we've accumulated? Whew.

Many of our past experiences will be indelible for all their glory. Our memories of the great moments are absolutely golden: A favorite old family dog, an "A" on a spelling test, a trip to the circus, a holiday get-together, a birthday party, a first car, a first kiss, a favorite song.

The past is a valuable part of who we are today. What we *do* about our unique experiences of yesteryear is up to us. Our past can be a heavy anchor, weighing us down and holding us back, if we let it. You've heard people blame their circumstances for not living up to their potential:

"I didn't have a good enough education."
"My parents were too poor."
"I was never popular."
"There were no good jobs around."
"My family was too dysfunctional."
"Nobody gave me a chance."

I had the pleasure of meeting the talented talk-show host and author, Larry King. He is SO good at what he does, I think, because he's curious. He really wants to know what all his guests have to say. Larry loves to learn. He's talked to all types of people; presidents, actors, agents, authors, magicians, musicians, multiple personalities ... you name it.

And he's a regular guy from Brooklyn. Never attended college. But Larry King persevered in the school of hard knocks to supreme success. No excuses.

HOME ON WHEELS

Speaking of the past, I do have some treasured memories of our trailer years.

That tiny space meant that we'd be together ... *really* together. There was no running off upstairs, or to the den, or to the separate kitchen. It was one little house on wheels, but I remember us laughing a lot. There were lots of fun times.

We can take the past, the bitter with the better, for what it is. The past. No need to try to live in it but rather learn from it. Think back to an experience that could have been a burden for you ... but was a blessing in disguise. Something that you can only appreciate in looking at the bigger picture over time.

If there's something you regret, consider it a powerful learning tool. Instead of "if only I had," you can say "now I can!"

*"People are always blaming
their circumstances
for what they are.
I don't believe
in circumstances.
The people who get on
in this world are the people
who get up and look for the
circumstances they want,
and, if they can't find them,
make them."*

George Bernard Shaw

THE FUTURE

Since the future's not here yet, I don't want us to spend too much of our precious time focusing on it. Like the past, the future is important, however. After all, goals are plans for future moments. Keeping our sights set on goals helps to keep us fired up!

It's difficult to really appreciate the present if we have no clue about the future ... no plans. To be responsible, we've got to have an idea, a picture, a plan of action for our lives on down the line. That's why we need to balance out living "now" and planning for "then."

Remember earlier in this chapter we mentioned those who *live* in the future? That's what we want to avoid. That keeps us from "now." And that's where worry lives. Worry steals away the magic of the present moment.

"Worry never changed one moment of history!"

CGA

Action changes things. Worry is vague anxiety about something that hasn't even happened. You need to let go of it ... it can rob your energy and spirit. If you have reasonable concern about something ... ACT on it ... then release it.

The more you practice being in this moment, the less you'll worry.

Whether you're in a happy or sad state, feel your feelings. You'll have a better measure of where you are and what you need. If you need help and emotional support, by all means get it. Ask around for the most professional help available. You're worth it. It could change your life.

REVIEW

NOW is the time to get fired up!

THE PRESENT - This is it, folks! Not yesterday. Not tomorrow. NOW. Be here. This is where it's all happening. The present is really all the time we're sure of. Practice getting more focused on it. ENJOY all of it. When you live in the present, you'll notice more about yourself and the world around you. The present will be brighter and so will your future. You'll be fully alive!

THE PAST - It's over and done. Your past is unique to you. Use the rich lessons it has taught you. It's part of who and what you are today. Embrace your past … but don't stay stuck there.

THE FUTURE - Plan for it. This is where your dreams and goals will be realized. But don't get stuck here either. Remember that "future-living" keeps you from the here and now. Worry is a vague anxiety about the future and has no value. Let go of it and take *action* instead.

CHAPTER FOUR

MAKE IT HAPPEN

"Inside every one of us
there's greatness to be born
like a flower always starts with just a seed.
Your life is like a movie
up on the silver screen
and only you can ever play the lead."

"Make it happen for your dreams.
Make it happen from your heart.
Right up to the end
make it happen from the start.
If you reach out today
and give it your best shot.
Make it happen for yourself.
Give it all you've got."

Anderson/McCree

We're all loaded with potential. So what? My Dad always says, "it doesn't amount to a hill of beans" if we don't DO something. That's true.

We can have everything it takes to plant an abundant garden: seeds, soil, water, a hoe, fertilizer, sunshine, everything. But, if we don't take action there's nothing happening. Except weeds.

There might be shelves of books all around us ... but if we don't reach out for one of those books, open it, and soak up the information, it's useless.

We have to *make* something happen with the powerful amount of potential we all have. Wouldn't it be a different scenario if Henry Ford gave up on the Model T after just a few tries? Because he kept his passion and perseverance, he contributed to greater convenience for all of us. In fact, now most families own at least two cars. That mobility changed a lot about our lifestyles.

HOPE HELPS TO MAKE IT HAPPEN

A friend of mine is a pilot with the Air National Guard, along with working in the music industry. Back in the 1980s, we'd get together now and then and talk shop about the music and publishing business.

Bob would often mention that he and a business partner, Pam Lewis, were working with a new country music act. He said he felt this developing singer would be a huge success.

I'd always wish him luck, knowing how difficult it is to be a huge success in any business, much less the crazy music biz.

Months would go by before I'd run into Bob again. "How's it going with that new singer you're working with?" I'd ask.

"Oh, it's coming along ... slowly but surely. But, he's gonna be big!" he'd answer.

At least a year later, I ran into my friend at a local showcase for new performers. It's a way to get experience and some exposure, usually limited. I asked Bob again how he was doing.

"I'm still working with that new artist," he'd answer.

"So, what's happening? Any updates?" I asked.

"Not yet, but he's gonna make it. He's gonna be big. In fact, could I introduce you to him? He's sitting in the back."

"Sure," my friends and I agreed.

Minutes later Bob presented this humble hopeful, who politely removed his cowboy hat to meet us.

"Folks, I'd like you to meet Garth Brooks."

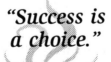

"Success is a choice."

CGA

*"Nothing contributes
so much to
tranquilize the mind
as a steady purpose ...
a point on which the soul
may fix its intellectual eye."*

Mary Wollstonecraft Shelley

To make it happen, we don't have to add a lot more "busy-ness" to our lives. We're plenty busy right now! What we need to do is prioritize our lives. To focus more on the really important things. This isn't much different from cleaning out a closet; sorting everything and keeping the good stuff ... letting go of what's become clutter.

In order to figure out what's most valuable to us, we have to take a personal inventory. We can categorize this inventory into several areas I mentioned in the first chapter: Work. Family. Health. Purpose.

For example ... ask yourself, "How can I really make it happen, on a greater scale, at work? What can I do that would add value? What are some talents I'm not using? Am I passionate about my work? Could I get passionate about it, or should I work toward doing something else?" Refer back to Chapter Two about loving your job.

Ask yourself, "How can I make it happen in my family life? What would raise the quality AND quantity of our time together? What specifics can I do to make an improvement this week? How far am I willing to go to make this a reality? How important is this, anyway? Maybe we can all get fired up!"

If your friends are your primary relationship, make them more of a priority. Nuture the relationships.

Your health is vital, too. When we're not feeling well, not much else matters at the time. Our health will make itself a priority, perhaps too late, if we don't. How can we make good health happen? Ask, "How am I feeling ... physically and emotionally? Do I look healthy and vibrant? Do I have plenty of energy? Is there a nagging problem that should be checked by a professional? Do I have regular check-ups just to be on the safe side? Am I getting enough rest and exercise?"

---

*"I keep the telephone of my mind
open to peace, harmony,
health, love and abundance.
Then whenever doubt, anxiety
or fear try to call me, they
keep getting a busy signal
and soon they'll forget my number."*

Edith Armstrong

Next, sense of purpose. See how much attention you're paying to the higher things of life. Ask yourself, "Am I giving back as well as taking? Can I make a difference in this world? What is my philosophy of life? Do I have a purpose here? Am I having a relationship with God or other Higher Power? Where do I fit in the big picture? Do I seek answers from those I respect? What comes after this life?"

THE WAVE PLAN

So, *how* do we actually make it happen? The WAVE plan. It's a compilation of actions we can take that have a good track record. All of the steps work individually and as a group ... done together.

Think of the individual instruments in a symphony. Each is unique and beautiful in its own way. But when those individual instruments are blended together ... wow! A bouquet of sound.

I call it the WAVE plan so it's easy to remember. It's an acronym for:

> *Write out goals.*

> *Affirm.*

> *Visualize.*

> *Experience.*

Many experts have sung the praises of writing out goals, affirming and visualizing for years. They DO work.

I've added "experience" to the list. It's important that we become more mindful of ourselves and our lives. Then we know what needs changing or what needs to be experienced and enjoyed more fully.

When you take action on all four of them, as a whole plan, the results are even more powerful!

WRITE OUT GOALS

Something happens when we actually write out our goals. As I mentioned in Chapter One, when we write out our goals, it's as though we really mean business. The act of writing them down helps to get them much more focused and crystallized in our minds. That's where action begins. Remember, our thoughts drive our actions.

Here are SIX STEPS to serious, long-range goal-setting:

1. IDENTIFY YOUR GOALS. What do you love to do ... where time seems to stand still? If money weren't an issue, what would you be doing? What do you want to accomplish ... now and down the road?

2. GATHER INFORMATION. What do you need to reach this goal? Find out all you can. Ask about it, read about it. Do lots of research.

3. LIST THE BENEFITS of reaching this goal. Think of every area of your life that could be improved by reaching your goal. Be specific.

4. LIST THE CHALLENGES. What are some realistic obstacles you'll need to overcome? How will you do that? If our goals were completely without challenge, we'd have been there by now. They should require us to keep growing and stretching.

5. PLAN YOUR ACTION. What specific steps will you take to reach your goal? Success comes from the culmination of each step. One step at a time we complete long, long journeys.

6. CREATE YOUR TIMETABLE. Write out a clear time-frame for each step of your goal. This acts as a goal-post. A marker of how you're moving along.

Now, GO FOR IT. Start today. Take action. And don't give up! Successful people are not more talented or lucky ... they're simply *doing* it. "Quit" isn't in their dictionary.

Chart your progress. Notice each positive step you're taking. Re-adjust and re-evaluate as you go along. Flexibility allows your goals to grow along with you.

"By the mile, it's a trial.
By the yard, it's hard.
But by the inch
It's a cinch."

Unknown

AFFIRM

To affirm is to strongly assert ... to confirm ... to declare. When we affirm ourselves, some powerful results happen. Here's why; the mind has three levels: the conscious, the subconscious, and the unconcious.

When we tap into the subconscious, we can allow information to seep into our conscious minds. The subconscious is a lot like a robot. It believes anything we tell it. What we fill that subconscious level with is of *vital* importance then.

If we tell our subconscious mind that we're stupid, embarrassed, not mechanical, not creative, impatient, always late, always wrong, too old, too sick, too scared, too tired ... or anything else, our subconscious mind believes it. Takes it in as fact. Period.

By the same token, if we tell this part of our mind that we're naturally bright, creative, energetic, healthy, open-minded, confident, loving, curious, adventurous, worthy, valuable, growing, etc., our subconscious mind believes all that. The subconscious believes *whatever* we repeatedly tell it.

We get to choose most of what that robot hears and believes. If that part of our mind has heard mostly negative comments, from ourselves or others, we can overpower it. We can replace those old, negative, hold-us-back thoughts with fresh, new, positive, exciting and empowering ones.

Gradually, what that subconscious level hears as fact, will begin to permeate the conscious mind. That's where we can become aware of and experience these thoughts. Where we can come to know them. If we flood that subconscious level with good, powerful affirmations, that's what we will begin to experience in our consciousness.

Affirmations can bring some huge results.

There are FOUR GUIDELINES to follow in order to make valuable affirmations. They should be:

1. PERSONAL

2. PRESENT TENSE

3. POWERFUL

4. PERSISTENT

Here are some examples: "I am successful." "I have abundance in all things." "I've got great goals and I'm reaching them now." "I feel better than ever." "I'm as valuable as any other person on the planet." "I was born with great talents and I'm using them now to make a difference." "I have enough time for the real important things."

Sports figures are notorious affirmers; Muhammed Ali got everyone's attention when, as a young boxer, he declared, "I am the greatest!" Back then, nobody had ever heard of this young guy from Louisville, Kentucky.

He kept saying it in every interview ... "I am the greatest!" At first, I thought he was crazy. He sure made a believer out of me.

Notice how that short statement, "I am the greatest!", fits all the criteria for a good affirmation:

It's **personal** ... starting out with "I".

It's in the **present tense** ... I AM. Not I *might* be ... not I *will* be.

It's **powerful** ... Ali didn't say, "I'm pretty darn good." He said, "I am the *greatest!*"

He was **persistent**. He repeated it again and again. Day after day.

By affirming himself so powerfully, Ali really began to believe it. And that belief made it happen. He became the boxing champion of the world! All his opponents had spent many hard, long hours in training ... just as Ali had. I believe that affirming gave him the winning edge.

"Believe it.
Receive it."

CGA

SOME AFFIRMING TIPS

An easy way to remember your affirmations is to keep a list of them. While you're getting used to this terrific process, read them right off your list.

Keep your affirmations simple. One sentence for each one is enough.

Take a deep breath before saying your affirmations and give it gusto! Say them out loud. Stand in front of a mirror if possible. Say them like you mean them.

You may feel awkward saying something you don't fully believe at first. No problem. Stick with it. Soon the conscious mind will soak up all this good stuff ... and you *will* believe it.

Update your affirmations as they become reality. Create new ones to keep up with your goals.

Affirm yourself often. First thing in the morning, during a work break, before you fall asleep, while you're driving, every chance you can to make it happen.

"Whatever the mind can
conceive and believe,
the mind can achieve."

Napoleon Hill

VISUALIZE

A picture is worth a thousand words. We've heard that forever because it makes so much sense. A picture is rich with great detail. We may have boxes, drawers, and albums full of pictures. Those images often conjure up a memory of an experience. Lots of those images are from positive experiences ... that's why I wonder why they're printed from "negatives." That's a joke. Are you paying attention? (I hear you groaning from here.)

To visualize is simply to create a picture in your mind. The more specific the better. This is a powerful process toward goal-getting. To picture every detail of the successful outcome.

Visualizing is so powerful it has helped many prisoners of war get through their ordeal with flying colors. Some POWs have said they played a full round of golf every single day ... in their mind's eye. Some have visualized, page by page, writing a complete book. After their release, they only had to type it out and they had the finished product.

Many sports figures also use visualization to reach their goals. Mary Lou Retton, Olympic gold-medalist in gymnastics, is a firm believer. She has said that she created a detailed visualization of winning at the Olympics ... and repeated it at least ten thousand times. She would picture the whole experience: the scoreboard showing a "10", the audience cheering, every facet of it ... even the endorsements that would follow!

---

*"If you think you can
or if you think you can't ...
you're right."*

Henry Ford

Visualizing can work in everyday situations too; My sister Lynn and I were driving toward a large mall to pick up a gift. It was pouring rain. As we got closer, we could see the parking lot was full. "Just for fun, let's visualize and affirm a great parking space," I said.

Cars were lined up near the doorways hoping for a breakthrough. As we got close to the main doorway, the car right next to us, in the very first space, put on its reverse lights and slowly started backing out. We couldn't move any other way, except to slip into that prime space. We still chuckle about that.

The key to visualizing your goals is to be specific. If your goal is to accept a new job, while you're taking action to get it, picture everything about it ... a great interview, a smooth, pleasant commute, meeting wonderful co-workers, a comfortable workspace, an opportunity to use your valuable strengths, a paycheck that reflects your worth and covers your financial responsibilities with some extra to save. Yes, this is possible!

Along with writing out goals, affirming and visualizing, there's one more that I feel is vital:

EXPERIENCE IT FULLY

It can be soooo easy to go through the entire day and wonder where it went. Has this ever happened to you? Often we get into that "future-living" mode I talked about earlier. Time has flown by and we remember little about it.

Why? We've raced through time. We didn't notice those moments going by because WE WEREN'T THERE. We didn't slow down enough to get into the present tense ... the "now." We didn't really experience the day. It buzzed right on by us. We let that happen. We missed the day and it will never come back. That's major!

---

*"Turn your
goal-setting into
goal-getting!"*

CGA

What good is reaching our goals if we don't fully appreciate and experience the successful outcome? We can get into the habit of becoming more mindful, aware of the present. It takes a little practice ... refer back to Chapter Three.

If we apply "Present Power" to our goal-reaching, we can truly and fully enjoy the results. Life is a series of moments. Savor the moments with all your senses.

I have a friend whose goals were to spend more time with his family and raise his income to $100,000 per year. Right now, his income has jumped to $150,000.

"Are you enjoying your financial success and spending more time with your family ... your two goals?" I asked.

"I think that when I reach the $200,000 mark, I'll relax and have more time to spend with my wonderful family," he said.

You see how we can let our accomplishments slip right through our hands and keep racing for more? My friend could afford plenty of time for the important things now, but he and his family are missing out. What a loss.

When you reach every success ... big and small ... honor it, feel it, notice each detail of it, give yourself a pat on the back, then move on. Don't wait until things are "perfect" ... you'll wait forever.

The WAVE plan can work for you. It can change your life if you MAKE IT HAPPEN. Believe in yourself, your goals, and your success. Experience life fully. And ENJOY where you are right now.

REVIEW

We can MAKE IT HAPPEN by following the "**WAVE**" plan:

WRITE OUT GOALS. Follow the six steps:

1. Identify your goals.
2. Gather information.
3. List the benefits of reaching the goal.
4. List the challenges.
5. Plan your action.
6. Create a timetable.

AFFIRM. The four guidelines:

Personal
Present tense
Powerful
Persistent

VISUALIZE. Be specific. Use all your senses.

EXPERIENCE the results fully.

CHAPTER FIVE

IT'S UP TO YOU

"You can reach... or you can rust.
And see your dreams just turn to dust.
Or you can break those chains
and make a change.
Let perfection step aside.
There's no room to be perfect
on this ride.
Whatever you do ... just remember
it's up to you.

It's up to you if you want to
give it all you've got.
Or hide behind excuses, fears and doubts.
It's up to you to go out there
and be all you can be.
'Cause you can make a difference starting now.
Whatever you do ... just remember
it's up to you!"

Carol Grace Anderson

A few years ago I spent several weeks in England filming some TV specials for the BBC (British Broadcasting Corporation). What a rich, fun, unforgettable experience.

An interesting highlight happened one evening while we were all in a meeting with the producers about the next day's shooting schedule. This meeting was on the top floor, the fourth, of Ye Olde King's Head Inn, an historic, quaint hotel near Horsham, England.

Soon after this meeting started, a female bobby (police officer) appeared at the door. In a very British accent, she said with controlled panic, "This is a bomb scare."

The woman was so polite, we thought she must be kidding. When nobody seemed to budge, she repeated the same message, "This IS a bomb scare. You must clear the premises at once."

Now we all looked at each other and thought she just might be for real. The reactions of the group varied widely:

"I can't leave, I'm waiting for a call from my boyfriend in the U.S."

"We better get the heck out of here quick!"

"Doesn't this happen all the time? What's the big deal?"

"We might all explode. Head for cover!"

"Find a few bottles of wine. Let's have a party," a crew member said.

One of the musicians said, "Grab the guitars, let's put on a free concert in the parking lot."

The CONDITIONS were all the same. Everyone was involved in a bomb scare. The DECISIONS about those conditions were all different, however. That's what this chapter is about. (And, by the way, we all left the building, it was searched and nothing was found. We did have a jam session in the parking lot ... a great time.)

Next time you're sitting in traffic, notice the different ways people deal with that same condition; some are *fuming*, some are enjoying a few extra minutes of peace and quiet, some are listening to music, some are making calls, some are scolding their kids, some are sipping coffee, some are daydreaming.

How you react to traffic is UP TO YOU. In fact, how you deal with your own unique blend of circumstances that make up all facets of your life ... is up to you. You choose.

Obstacle?	**Opportunity?**
Win?	**Lose?**
Give?	**Give up?**
Reach?	**Rust?**
Hurt?	**Heal?**
Sink?	**Swim?**
Fear?	**Faith?**
Try?	**Triumph?**

ATTITUDE

Attitude is one of the most valuable, important, and powerful tools we can discuss. And it's FREE and AVAILABLE to everyone.

Psychologist Dr. Karl Menninger said, "Attitude is more important than facts." I thought that *sounded* profound but I never really got a grip on the power of that statement. That is, until I saw an interview of a man newly delegated to a wheelchair ... Christopher Reeve. He was smiling a lot, too. That's a wow!

By the way, to *all* of you who are smiling and full of hope and plans in the darkest of circumstances ... that's the essence of a positive attitude. Thank you for your powerful example and message.

The experts in anatomy say that we humans have, literally, many *billions* of brain cells. Can you imagine the results we can generate when we put many of those cells in a positive frame of thought? Again, our thoughts lead to our feelings, which lead to our actions.

On the other hand, we can turn our attitude into a negative force through the power of our thoughts. Dr. Norman Vincent Peale gave a great example of this:

He and his wife were in Hong Kong. While she was shopping, he ambled down the street and walked past a tattoo parlor. Fascinated, he looked in the window at all the intricate designs and slogans.

One particularly caught his eye. It said, "Born to lose."

Dr. Peale asked the proprietor why someone would want a permanent message like that on their arm.

He replied, "Before tattoo on body, tattoo on mind."

"Powerful thoughts lead to powerful actions."

CGA

The thoughts we create in our minds can make or break us. The good news is we can control our thoughts. Think about it! Even if we've had a terribly sad childhood ... even if we were given unloving messages ... even if we've had some serious challenges as adults ... we can replace those negative messages with positive ones. We can overpower them. Zap them out of existence.

THE DAILY CLEAN SLATE

We can *choose* a GREAT attitude. We can start right this very minute. Every morning of our lives is a new day. It's like a big blank screen. We're the ones who will write the script for the day. We're the directors. The authors. The CEOs of our lives.

We decide how we're going to fill the day. Who we'll spend time with. What kind of outlook we'll have. What our priorities will be. How we'll take care of our responsibilities ... including ourselves. Whether we'll experience humor or torment. Peace or anxiety. Serenity or stress.

Each one of us fills in all the blanks, all the possibilities of each day. We start with a big, blank screen.

BLANK SCREEN/SILVER SCREEN

In the early 1990s, an agent asked if I would audition for a movie Paramount was filming, THE THING CALLED LOVE. The small role was for a tall, southern waitress. At 5'11", I knew I had the "tall" covered. And I have been a waitress, so I showed up ... got in line with the many other hopefuls.

The audition seemed to go pretty well. I gave them the best southern drawl I could muster. A week later, I had what they refer to as a "call-back." Now I had to read some of the lines in the script to the Hollywood producer, Peter Bogdanovich.

Again, it was fun and seemed to go well. I didn't hear anything and forgot all about it. Then two weeks later, the same agent called again and said, "You got it! Can you be on the set next Monday for a wardrobe fitting?"

In total shock, I agreed. This was thrilling. Unreal.

The first day, they showed me to "my trailer." (It felt so familiar.) There was a star on the door under my name and everything. I took several pictures of it, of course.

I was then led to the make-up area and was introduced to the other actor in my scenes. Sandra and I would spend hours waiting for just the right camera angles, lighting, blocking, and then rehearsing our scenes. Over and over again.

It was clear she *loved* what she was doing. Her attitude was outstanding all the time ... at three in the afternoon, or three in the morning. She was lots of fun to be around. It was also clear that she was very gifted.

When my scenes had all been shot, I said goodby and told her I never got her full name. "Oh, let's stay in touch. This was fun. My name's Sandra Bullock."

It was 5:30 in the morning. A soft rain was falling. This movie stuff was exhausting.

Of course Sandra Bullock went on to star in huge blockbusters. She is *very* talented and beautiful ... but I think her great attitude makes her even more bankable.

SEVEN STEPS TO A GREAT ATTITUDE

So, how do we *get* a great attitude? Not all of us were born with a naturally positive, optimistic attitude. But, I believe if you follow these SEVEN STEPS, you'll greatly improve yours. And if you follow these steps with conviction for 21 days, I *guarantee* you'll see an attitude improvement. That's a strong statement, but we have to take action for results.

1. POSITIVE PEOPLE. Surrounding yourself with positive people whenever possible feels good. It's uplifting. A great attitude is contagious. That's why those success rallies are so successful! We want what they've got. We want to get fired up. And it's possible.

Are your friends dragging you down? Are your co-workers wallowing in hopelessness, gossip, and negativism? Does your family seem zoned out and isolated?

Since family is most important, start there first. Ask yourself what your part in this humdrum unit might be? What can you do to contribute to turning things around? To get the process moving?

It takes commitment because it takes time. You could begin with planning some activities they'd like. Get their feedback. If you have teenagers, they might not like anything you like ... too geeky. But plan something you think they'd like once it got going. They might even honor your effort. Schedule it in. Get support from your spouse or friends. Keep at it.

About your friends. If they're not full of life, support, and action, ask yourself why you'd spend your precious time with them. Aren't you worth more? Isn't your time more valuable?

Since we choose our friends, and friendships are important, make an effort to find positive, upbeat ones. You can get to know them at clubs where you have a mutual interest; at church where there's a common belief system; in your neighborhood by getting more acquainted with the folks around you. Being open to it makes a difference.

What about co-workers? If they're full of negative energy, that can easily permeate your attitude. It has an effect on your physical state, too. Even the output of the total organization is effected.

You've walked into a business and sensed a negative vibe immediately. Right? That's how obvious it can be. Even an outsider can spot it ... sometimes easier than the insider who doesn't seem to notice anymore.

Your options? Make an effort toward finding the good apples in your organization. Get to know them. Or, spend more time on your own, keeping your great attitude in place. Or, see if you can bring others onto your bandwagon. If all else fails, you can always look into getting another job with a more positive outlook and environment. They're out there.

2. INSPIRING BOOKS. What we fill our minds with is reflected in everything we do. Filling up on wonderful books is great nourishment for the attitude. Reading one a week can do wonders.

Most bookstores have large selections of titles for self-improvement, success, personal development ... all in one area. Of course, The Bible is loaded with helpful guidelines.

Libraries have entire sections devoted to these topics also.

Borrow books from friends. Ask what they recommend. Positive thinkers usually have a nice collection of books on self-improvement.

One of my friends has just started a book club. We get together, bring a pot-luck supper, and share some info about a current book we've read. Then we loan the book to whoever shows interest.

"No time," you say? Rent these books on tape for your car. You'll be empowering yourself as you drive. Adding a smile by the mile!

3. MOTIVATIONAL TAPES. Many great motivational speakers have recorded specific tape programs. They usually come as a complete set. They can be pricey, but again, if you're committed, you can buy them as an investment with friends, borrow them, whatever it takes.

When you listen to these messages over and over, it overpowers so much negative we're all exposed to. Repetition is the key.

Three of my favorites are: *THE PSYCHOLOGY OF WINNING*, by Denis Waitley, *THE AWAKENED LIFE*, by Dr. Wayne Dyer, and *THE PSYCHOLOGY OF ACHIEVEMENT*, by Brian Tracy. In fact, I bought them four or five years ago and still listen to them. The above are all beneficial ... and there are many more.

Besides listening in the car, pop a tape in during a lunch break, while you're walking, wherever.

4. INSPIRING MUSIC. I feel that music, as much as anything on the planet, has a powerful effect on our overall feeling. That's why it's a billion dollar industry. That's why it's used in advertising, movies, TV, radio, elevators, grocery stores, weddings, parties, religious services of all kinds ... music is everywhere.

Music can make us feel up, down, melancholy, romantic, frantic, serene. It colors the environment we're in. Music can reflect our rebelliousness, our fine taste, our age group, our interests, our beliefs, our experiences.

"Music is the magic of the soul."

CGA

Haven't you heard music that brought tears to your eyes because it was so touching? Or uplifting? The lyrics said what you wanted or needed to hear. A song can be three minutes of heaven.

Filling our lives with *inspiring* music is a powerful way to get a great attitude. Where do you find it? Check out your local record store. Ask around. Listen to different samples to see what's best for you. There's some peaceful and uplifting instrumental music. And there's more and more music with inspirational lyrics available.

I wanted to hear contemporary, upbeat songs with a motivating message. I couldn't find exactly what I was looking for, so I co-wrote and recorded the ten-song collection, *YOU HOLD THE KEY!* Lyric samples open each chapter of this book. (See order form in back.)

5. STP - SELF-TALK POWER. If you keep telling yourself, "I'm *making* it a great day!" ... how could it be an awful day? Here are those affirmations again. They work.

Keep a running dialogue going in your mind. Talk out loud every chance you get, saying things like: "I feel great." "Wonderful things are going on in my life." "I'm making choices that bring the results I want." "I make time for the real important things." "I have a lot to offer and I now have many opportunities."

This self-talk is one of the very best ways to raise your self-esteem and confidence level! We can truly let go of those old messages that aren't doing us any good. They hold us back. They keep us in fear ... those "but what ifs." When we replace them with power thoughts, amazing things happen.

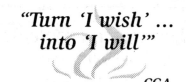

*"Turn 'I wish' ...
into 'I will'"*

CGA

6. ACT "AS IF". Something amazing happens when we act "as if" the outcome we're striving for is already here. If your goal is to have a great attitude and be filled with hope ... act "as if" you have a fantastic attitude now. Soon you will ... in a genuine way.

I've seen examples of a friend, very anxious about a situation or presentation, act "as if" he had all the solutions and confidence in the world. Again, the subconscious believes anything. When he started acting confidently ... he began to think that way. In some instances, you *can* put the cart before the horse.

Right now, I'm using this technique writing this book. Every page, I write "as if" you are already reading the completed book. If you're reading it, it's worked!

This acting "as if" works for financial success, too. Study the work habits of very successful people. They don't waste any time gossiping, complaining, moaning, and groaning. Instead, they're busy turning their dreams into reality. Act "as if" they're your peers.

"Losers see problems.
Winners see
possibilities!"

Unknown

---

7. LIST EVERYTHING GOING RIGHT! Experts report that we think approximately 60,000 thoughts per day. However, we can only think one thought at a time. Even if we jump from one thought to the next, it's still one thought at a time.

Imagine, then, the power of listing just the good stuff. While you're doing that, you can only focus on the positive. Your mind may want to wander back to the old, tired negative thoughts ... if that's what's most familiar. Keep reeling it back in to your list. You'll get used to it pretty fast. Especially when you experience the great feeling of noticing so many positive things. Things you might rarely, if ever, stop to notice or remember.

At first, it may seem difficult. If it's hard to think of even one thing to get started ... you *really* need this exercise. If you get stuck after 10 or 11 items, don't give up. Be patient with yourself. Write on!

Focus on things you're grateful for ... what you already have. You might start with something as broad as:

"Today I'm alive."

"I'm glad I have eyesight."

"I'm grateful for the roof over my head."

"I'm thankful for my mind."

"I appreciate my family."

"I'm grateful for air conditioning!"

"I didn't get run over by a Mack truck today."

"I'm glad remote controls were invented."

"Happiness is not something you find, but rather something you create."

Unknown

Use the space provided on the next two pages to get rolling. Refer back to your list every time you need an attitude adjustment. Make a new list every week or two to keep you on a positive track. In Chapter Ten we'll cover the power of a "Grateful Journal."

Some things going right are ...

1. _____

2. _____

3. _____

4. _____

5. _____

6. _____

7. _____

8. _____

9. _____

10. _____

11. _____

12. _____

13. _____

14. _____

15. _____

16. _____

17. _____

18. _____

19. _____

20. _____

Did you ever notice how happy people seem to be very grateful? There's a real correlation. Here's an example:

My Mom and Dad had a youth ministry, Jubilee Youth, in the Flatbush section of Brooklyn, N.Y. for many years. They operated a non-profit center where teenagers could drop by after school. The kids would have group discussions, take classes in art, music, leather work, woodworking; go on skating trips, hiking trips, etc. On Saturday nights, they had top-notch variety programs with an inspiring message. This all expanded their inner-city world.

A local Brooklyn woman named Isabella States heard about this and wanted to become involved. "Miss States" as we always called her had just retired as a secretary from Parke Davis Pharmaceutical Company. She offered to help out ... donating her bookkeeping and secretarial experience.

She got SO into it, she began to work fulltime. She stayed on board for nearly twenty years. Until she was stricken with cancer in her 80s. Never would take a penny for her years of hard work. Not one red cent.

"To love what you do and feel that it matters ... how could anything be more fun?"

Katharine Graham

Something else I want you to know about Miss States ... she always had a great attitude. For instance, she loved ice cream ... and to see her eyes twinkle when she'd dig into a strawberry ice cream cone was a real treat. Miss States showed us all how to treasure even the smallest things. She would probably celebrate the grand opening of a can of soup!

If you feel that creating or maintaining a positive attitude is just too hard, try visiting an emergency room waiting area for an hour or so. Also, volunteering at a kids' ward, or any ward of a hospital, should help you appreciate where you are ... and it works fast.

Getting and keeping a good attitude is a lot like working out. It requires regular attention. We don't expect to be in healthy, aerobic shape by taking one walk. It has to become part of our routine. The same with having a great attitude. One step at a time brings great results. Keeping at it is the key.

Following these seven simple steps will do wonders for your attitude. I promise.

REVIEW

Attitude? If you want to get fired up ... IT'S UP TO YOU!

Remember the **SEVEN STEPS** to a great attitude:

1. **POSITIVE PEOPLE.**
   Surround yourself with them.

2. **INSPIRING BOOKS.**
   Reading is powerful.

3. **MOTIVATIONAL TAPES.**
   Repetition makes a difference.

4. **INSPIRING MUSIC.**
   A fun attitude enhancer.

5. **STP - SELF-TALK POWER.**
   Affirm as often as possible.

6. **ACT "AS IF."**
   Act "as if" you have a great attitude.

7. **LIST EVERYTHING GOING RIGHT!**
   You'll be amazed.

CHAPTER SIX

YOU HOLD THE KEY

"You hold the key to get your engine goin'.
Now put it into gear and get your sweet self rollin'.
It doesn't matter how you get there
as long as you go.

You hold the key to everything your thinkin'.
And you get to choose if you'll be sinkin' or swimmin'.
It's time to leave the dock and start
row, row, rowin' your boat."

Carol Grace Anderson

Keys have always been fascinating to me. Since I was a kid, I saved every key I could. I now have a big box full of keys. It would be interesting to know what they unlocked in their heyday.

Did you ever lose your keys? Ever lock yourself out of your car? Your house? Talk about a major inconvenience. That's how important keys are. They give us access to valuable things.

TRYING TO CRACK THE GREAT KEY CASE

Last year I picked up a friend from the airport who had a meeting near my office. I offered to take him back to the airport after his meeting. In fact, on the way back, since he had a similar car, I asked if he would drive to see if my car was pulling to the right.

He gladly agreed, and asked if he could pick up some papers from another office on the way. No problem.

I waited in the car. When he returned, he attempted to put the key back in the ignition. It wouldn't go more than half way. After many attempts, I gave it a try. Nothing. That key wouldn't budge.

After a half-hour of working on any possible solution, with the same result, I suggested he get a cab. No sense in missing his flight. I called a locksmith.

He arrived soon after and I explained the strange key mystery to him hoping for the missing clue. He said, "Ma'am, I don't fix 'em. I just replace 'em." And so he did. I now had a new ignition switch and a new key that fit perfectly.

On the way back to my office, I made a quick stop at a convenience store. Returning, I started to put the key in the door lock and realized it wouldn't go more than half way. Again! In disbelief, I tried the door on the passenger side. Same thing.

I called the same locksmith again. He said he'd be right there. What a valuable customer I was ... calling for service twice in about twenty minutes. It was almost laughable.

While I waited, sitting on the curb in the quiet parking lot, the answer came to me: Those were not my keys. They just *looked* like them. They were actually my friend's keys. Remember, he had the same type car. He had inadvertently pulled his keys out of his pocket when he re-started my car. That was my theory.

That evening, my friend called to say that when he landed, his keys wouldn't fit the ignition to his car. He came up with the same conclusion. After many apologies and covering the locksmith expenses, he still can't get over the complication. Small keys, big hassle.

KEYS ARE SIGNIFICANT

Now that we know how to get a great attitude, it's important to go to the next step ... TO UNLOCK OUR BEST.

Just as each key may unlock a different door, each one of us was given a unique and valuable stash of gifts and talents at birth. That is our potential. We've got tons of it. Most of it we're not aware of because it's never been uncovered.

WE ARE ACCOUNTABLE for what we do, or don't do, with these individual gifts of potential. This is where we hold the key.

SHE PLAYS 88 KEYS

My Mom is a gifted musician ... a natural talent on the piano and organ. She's also a master at improvising and arranging. At age 71 she recorded her first album: *WHISPERS OF LOVE*. Mom did the whole thing without one piece of music. It was all out of her head ... and incredibly beautiful.

Although my mother was born with this potential, she started taking lessons when she was six. Her little legs were too short to reach the pedals so they just dangled. During the winter, she'd practice in the cold, unheated living room until her fingers would get too numb to feel the keys.

By the time Mom was 12, she was playing in church and creating her own hymn arrangements.

Then as a teenager, she'd take a train from southern New Jersey into New York to study with a master teacher in a studio at Carnegie Hall. (I love that old joke: "How do you get to Carnegie Hall?" Answer: "Practice! Practice! Practice!") To help fund those lessons, she'd give piano lessons to beginners in her neighborhood.

Mom is now 78 and still gives up to 39 individual piano lessons a week. And they're all house calls ... she drives to their homes.

SOME KEY QUESTIONS

To help unlock the treasure chest of your special gifts, here are some powerful questions. Brian Tracy posed them in his tape set, *THE PSYCHOLOGY OF ACHIEVEMENT.* Answer the following:

1. What are your three most important life goals?

a. _____

b. _____

c. _____

2. If you had only six months to live, what would you be doing?

_____

3. What have you always wanted to do but were afraid to?

_____

4. What five things in life are most important to you?

a. _____

b. _____

c. _____

d. _____

e. _____

5. What would you do if you won a million dollars?

_____

6. What activity gives you the greatest feeling of self-worth?

_____

7. If you could receive one magic gift, what would it be?

_____

A valuable and fun activity would be to discuss these questions with your family and friends. Answering these questions can give you goal-clarity. Getting focused is vital to moving ahead. First you want an idea of where you really want to go. Here's some help:

SUCCESS AT ANYTHING ... IN 3D

1. DECIDE what you want to do with your wonderful, gifted, self. We kicked this book off in Chapter One with the importance of taking that first step of deciding. What's holding you back? If you look closely, you'll see that goal-stealer, fear, lurking around somewhere.

Those old messages may creep in: "Oh, you can't do that ... what are you crazy?" "It's never been done that way before." "Leave it to the experts." "Why bother?" "It's better to be safe than sorry."

You know those who say, "I'd like things to be different, but it's impossible." "I'm stuck". "There's no way out." "I have no options." These are people who truly believe life must be not only difficult but thoroughly miserable to boot! And our *beliefs* create our reality.

Yes, we achieve what we believe. The first way to change these thoughts and get on track is to *decide* what we're going to do.

One way to do that is to look at our past decisions. I was surprised when I created a list of all the jobs I've had. It was a wild, roundabout journey to get to the present. Here they are in sequence:

Greeting card sales (age 6) ... door to door
Running errands for neighbors
Soloist on my Dad's local TV show
Clerk in a 5&10 cent store
Clerk in a dairy store
House cleaner (*my* room never got the benefit)
Waitress
Cook (for up to 250 people)
Ceramics instructor
Horseback riding instructor
Locker room attendant and cleaner
Babysitter (over 500 hours during college)
Teacher
Counselor
Songwriter
Limo driver (I carried *their* luggage.)
Office temp
Background singer
Actress
Publicist
Speaker
Author

In looking over this list, I wonder what I'll do when I grow up. I also see how each job was a key step in my journey ... whether it was short-term, to pay the rent ... or preparing me for something I needed much later.

The sacrifice of not having children made this list a lot longer than it would have been. But I think we should teach the younger generation to honor many options, too. It's enriching. And now nearly unavoidable. We have to be prepared ... and more flexible than ever before.

The days of starting out with one company and staying until retirement are history. It used to be the rule. Since the entire business world is changing, so is our workstyle. We're more challenged than ever to use more of our skills and talents. I think that's a plus in the long run.

You may be having a more direct trip in your job history. Your list will give you some interesting and relevant information. It can help you decide where you want to go.

2. DISCOVER ALL THE POSSIBILITIES. We can thank the great inventors for this. Because they looked beyond the ordinary, we all enjoy the benefits. Electric refrigeration, heating systems, cars, planes, medical breakthroughs, telecommunication, you name it.

To help you in deciding what you really want to do, discover all the possibilities you can. For starters, make a list of everything you're pretty good at. Begin here:

_____   _____

_____   _____

_____   _____

_____   _____

Here's a small sampling of ideas:

Math	Painting
Mechanics	Cooking
Selling	Driving
Building	Tailoring
Computers	Organizing
Landscaping	Typing
Singing	Caregiving
Teaching	Writing
Performing	Decorating

Now give your long list a close look. See if the jobs you've had in your lifetime match up with your talents. If not, why not?

You hold the key. Go beyond what's ordinary for you and see what you can do. Now that you've got a better idea of the many things you're good at, see how you might apply them to improving your life.

FINDING YOUR TRUE PASSION

If money were not an issue, what would you be doing? When you're involved in a project where time seems to fly ... when it's more fun than work ... that's passion.

We've all seen musicians giving it all they've got. They're passionate about it. Often they love to jam in a living room (for free) just as much as on stage in front of thousands.

Ed Penney was a talented songwriter and producer but he had another passion ... a long-time hobby and love of collecting old books. He took that passion, left the music industry, and opened up a store selling valuable, old books. The business is now thriving after a few years of very hard work. He's enjoying every minute of it.

I stopped in to see Ed a few weeks ago. There he sat near the counter in a big, comfortable, easy chair, reading an old book. His eyes were smiling as he told me how much he loves what he's doing.

Discover your possibilities and do what you love. Even if you can only do it part time. It could work into something more. You'll make a real contribution to the world.

"Nothing in the world can take the place of persistence.
Talent will not;
nothing is more common than unsuccessful men with talent.
Genius will not;
unrewarded genius is almost a proverb.
Education will not;
The world is full of educated derelicts.
Persistence and determination alone are omnipotent."

Calvin Coolidge

---

3. DEVOTE YOURSELF TO IT. Once you DECIDE and DISCOVER THE POSSIBILITIES then DEVOTE. Following through when the road gets rough takes devotion. Whatever it is in life ... relationships, parenting, work, good health, success ... they all take dedication.

Roy Clark was truly devoted to learning to play the guitar ... and to play it well. When he was 14, his parents gave him a Silvertone model guitar from Sears for Christmas.

He'd take that guitar up to his room above the kitchen and practice the chords his Daddy showed him. He practiced them over and over and over again. He couldn't hear his Mama calling him for supper, so she'd pound on the kitchen ceiling with a broom handle.

When he'd finally hear her, he'd come to the table with his fingers all wrapped up. They were literally bleeding.

He kept at it. Those tender fingertips soon developed calluses, making it much more comfortable to play. To this day, Roy plays the guitar as much as ever. He's happy to say he still has calluses.

Clark became one of the greatest and most awarded entertainers in country music history ... a result of talent *and* devotion.

Here's a simple equation for this:

PASSION + PERSEVERANCE = *PLENTY!*

Again the 3D's are: DECIDE what you want to do.
DISCOVER all the possibilities. DEVOTE yourself to it.

SO WHAT'S HOLDING YOU BACK?

If it sounds so simple, why isn't everyone doing it? For
one reason, it's those old messages again. We hear them
everywhere. Even in public schools, we're strongly
encouraged to fit in; to be like everyone else; to move along
at a prescribed pace; "don't rock the boat." We weren't
encouraged to celebrate our uniqueness and go for it. No
way.

Albert Einstein didn't fit into the educational system at
all. He was described by his teacher as, "mentally slow,
unsociable, adrift forever in his foolish dreams."

Many great thinkers didn't fit in. In fact, current studies
show that there is no correlation between high achievement
in school and later success: Thomas Edison's teachers
thought he had a real learning disability. Walt Disney was
once told he didn't have enough good ideas and was fired
by a newspaper editor.

We're a society driven by the images we see on the
screen and in print. On TV, in movies, magazines,
billboards. Again, these images are telling us what to buy,
how to look, what to eat, where to go, who's in, who's out,
who's hot, who's not.

We might be holding ourselves back with the age-old
excuse of age. "I'd follow my heart and dreams if I were
younger." "It's too late to start now." The truth is, many

legendary artistic, medical, intellectual, or industrial breakthroughs were contributed by persons over 50! Many were much older. Here are some late bloomers:

George Burns finally won an Oscar at 80.
Michelangelo painted the Sistine Chapel at age 71.
Dr. Norman Vincent Peale was still speaking at age 94.
Grandma Moses started painting at 80.
Harlan Sanders founded the KFC chain after he was 65.

Wisdom comes with age. I wonder why the workforce is encouraged to "retire" at a certain age ... often around 65. This is when they're rich with experience. They've collected all this wisdom, then they're let go. I don't get it.

The elders I know feel great when they're busy and have a sense of purpose. Sure, a job change might be welcomed ... or a reduction of hours. In general, we humans enjoy being productive at any age. It feels good to help make a difference. Miss States, that "retired" secretary from Brooklyn, was a great example.

At every point in our lives, it's time to keep moving forward. Growing, exploring, enjoying.

EXPEL EXCUSES

To be our best, we have to buck the tide. We have to expel all excuses and take responsibility ... take action.

All the top-of-the-line workout equipment is not worth diddly if it just sits there. Every university campus is worthless without exchange of information going on. An entire field of wheat is useless unless it's harvested.

And to hold back *your* greatness is a loss to all of us.

Hopefully, we all have dreams. They're simply thoughts. Visions of success. And they can fuel our action. But we have to *do* something to get the engine cranked up ... turn the key.

You are unique and powerful. You have control over what you do with your life. Unlock your best and you *and* your loved ones will benefit. It's a win/win deal. Get fired up! YOU HOLD THE KEY.

"The difference between ordinary and extraordinary is that little extra."

Unknown

REVIEW

YOU HOLD THE KEY to your attitude, your actions, your achievements.

We asked **SEVEN KEY QUESTIONS:**

1. What are your three most important life goals?
2. If you had only six months to live, what would you be doing?
3. What have you always wanted to do but were afraid to?
4. What five things in life are most important to you?
5. What would you do if you won a million dollars?
6. What activity gives you the greatest feeling of self-worth?
7. If you could receive one magic gift, what would it be?

The **3D's** for unlocking your best:

DECIDE what you want to do.

DISCOVER all the possibilities.

DEVOTE yourself to it.

CHAPTER SEVEN

YOU CAN'T LEAD...
WHERE YOU WON'T GO

"You can't lead where you won't go
You can't teach what you don't know
You won't know about it 'til you try
If you don't change then you won't grow
You won't reap what you don't sow
And the chance to really live will pass you by

If you don't seek you'll never find
The pearls of wisdom in your mind
If you don't look you'll never really see
So let's sing for the world to hear
The song inside us loud and clear
A song of peace and love in harmony"

Anderson/McCree

"Actions speak louder than words." "Practice what you preach!" "Honesty is the best policy." You've heard 'em all. They've been around for ages because those old, familiar phrases are right.

In order to get truly fired up without burning out, we've got to be more honest with ourselves and others. Sounds simple. But I mean truly accountable and completely ethical.

I've heard the word "character" described as "what you would do in the dark with little chance of getting caught." It means moral excellence. Rightness. And it comes from within.

But how does character get there in the first place? We learn it from watching intentional and unintentional role models. We learn it from a general feeling of discomfort or even deep pain when we go against it. We learn it from the wisdom of growing. Some never learn it at all.

If we believe in ethics, in the Golden Rule, in the Ten Commandments, we've got to be accountable. We can't lead where we won't go.

"OFFICER, MAY I HAVE MY VOLKSWAGEN BACK?"

For the first time, I bought a shiny new car ... a creamy beige Volkswagen beetle with a chocolate-brown interior. Beautiful.

While I was teaching in the jail, I was taking courses at New York University to complete my Masters degree. How fun it was to buzz around the Big Apple in my bug. But, it was a time of lots of construction, making it nearly impossible to find a parking space.

My courses were in the evening and since the building crews were gone, I'd often park near the construction sites. There were signs that said "NO PARKING" but I'd be careful not to block any fire hydrants and park anyway. It felt safer to park right across the street from the class building.

Often, I'd return to my car after long classes and find a parking ticket on the windshield. Throwing it into the glove compartment, I'd take off and forget about it. "The city should provide more parking and I wouldn't have this problem!" I thought to myself.

After a couple semesters, I came out of class as usual one evening but saw no sign of my car. Nervously, I dialed 911 to alert the police of my stolen car. Who *wouldn't* want that tiny, shiny, lean machine that could go from here to Timbuktu on one tank of gas?

"What's the license plate number on your car, ma'am?"

"PJ 5217," I answered the police officer.

After what seemed like an eternity, the officer came back on the line and told me they *had* my car. Whew, was I relieved!

I asked for the address and told the cop I'd be right down to retrieve it.

"Sure, young lady ... but, uh, bring $2,900 cash or cashier's check with ya if you plan on taking your car outta here."

Shocked silence. I was truly speechless.

The officer went on to explain that the traffic cop who issued parking tickets ran a random computer check on my car after writing yet another ticket. It showed that those little "nuisance" violations I had accrued amounted to $2,900.

There was now a lien against my car.

Sure enough. He reminded me of the stack that had accumulated in my glove compartment ... the fines doubling and tripling over time.

Indignantly, I asked if I could pay it off in a series of payments. That was out of the question.

The seriousness of all this began to sink in. Not only was I too financially challenged to pay the huge fine ... I didn't have enough cash with me for bus fare to get home!

Walking in the cold rain toward the Port Authority bus station, I literally pan-handled for change.

Assessing the dismal results, I wasn't very good at it. I even tried to tell the details to total strangers ... that I was a teacher and just had my car towed. My long, blond hair at the time was drenched and matted from the rain. Mascara was meandering. I probably looked like a drowned rat looking for a drug fix.

Finally, a sweet old man in line at the ticket counter gave me the two dollars I needed for the bus ticket. He wouldn't tell me where to send the cash back to him.

SO, WHAT HAPPENED?

After a long struggle to fight city hall ... I lost. That means, the City of New York *sold* my car at a public auction. I attended. What a sad occasion. It brought enough for them to recover the fines but I still had to make the remaining car payments on it. And buy an old, battered up Chevy to get around in.

For a long time, I held a grudge against the NYPD. "How could they take my car and *sell* it over some lousy parking tickets?" But a few years ago, I assessed my own ethics. The light came on. I could see clearly that *I* was wrong all the way.

Wrong to park illegally.

Wrong to disregard traffic tickets.

Wrong to be unaccountable.

Even wrong to leave home without enough cash for an emergency.

It felt good, after many years, to finally admit my delinquency. By taking responsibility for my behavior, I felt empowered. It felt right and mature.

When we acknowledge our mistakes, it becomes easier to acknowledge our triumphs. We can look at our total selves more openly and honestly. If we don't believe we have any weaknesses, there's no room for change and improvement.

DOES IT PASS THE ETHICS TEST?

How do we know if something is right, wrong, ethical, unethical, good, bad, etc.? Here are six simple questions to help in that decision:

1. WILL IT HARM OTHERS OR MYSELF? Ask yourself if, by taking this action, you could cause physical, emotional, or spiritual harm to you or another person. Even participating in a conversation with gossip involved has negative consequences. This is not the same as telling a friend or relative directly that you are concerned about a behavior they're engaged in. That's responsible concern.

What we're talking about is stopping to take a beat and consulting our inner wisdom. What are some possible outcomes? You'll sense if something seems harmful or not.

2. IS IT FAIR? Of course, everything in life doesn't always appear to be fair and just. That doesn't take us off the hook. We have many choices and it's important for us to ask, "Is this really fair?"

The Olympic Games work diligently to create fair circumstances. Now they use a lot of new electronic devices to determine fair outcomes down to the thousandth of a second. That promotes objectivity. But something as subjective as the artistic marks for figure skating are much harder to judge. Personal preferences of the judges become involved. Fairness can be vague.

Why do you get flustered when someone ahead of you in the grocery express line has a full cart? Because it's not fair.

You can't control someone else's level of fairness, even a clearly bad call by a referree. You *can* control *your* choice of fairness.

3. DOES IT PASS THE FRONT PAGE TEST? Here's a good question to ask yourself in this right-or-wrong quiz. Would you be proud to have this action you're contemplating blazed across the front page of the newspaper?

Would you like your family and friends to get you some extra copies as keepsakes?

4. IS IT HONEST? The dictionary defines being honest as, "sincere, reliable, frank and open." It doesn't say it's easy. To be open and frank about yourself and others ... to live honestly ... takes guts. It's the essence of who you are.

The very first day I got my driver's permit at sixteen, I was driving my Mom into town, seven miles away. I had the radio blasting and was rocking right along. She reminded me that we were now in a slower, 45mph zone and I should slow down. I did for about five seconds, then went right back up to speed.

Out of the blue came a siren and flashing lights behind us. I pulled   over immediately. So did the policeman. He told me I was going 20mph over the speed limit. When my Mom said, "Yes, I told her to slow down ... she was going way too fast!" he wrote out my first ticket. It's still funny ... but she was honest.

5. DO I BELIEVE IN IT? Here's a good measurement. Deep in our core, we know if we truly believe in something or not. Sometimes a situation will come along that seems just a little shady or unethical. But with a good spin on it, it can be inviting. Often it sounds too good to be true. It ends up being a loser every time. Get-rich-quick schemes are a good example.

Psychic hotlines are making a fortune ... up to $4.00 per minute ... preying on those who *want* to believe. The callers are literally buying hope from complete strangers.

Religious cults thrive when there are enough members who ignore the red flags and buy the sales pitch.

It's best to keep our minds and hearts open ... staying in touch with our true beliefs and gut instincts.

6. IS IT RIGHT? A simple question. Taking a few pens or paperclips from work or making some personal long-distance calls doesn't seem like much, but is it right?

If the bank teller mistakenly overpays us by $10, is it okay to keep it? After all, the bank has plenty of money.

You bought several pieces of furniture and the store forgot to bill you for one expensive piece. Is it right to blow it off?

Of course not. But sometimes we encounter a tricky circumstance that may be honest, but not exactly right. Kids are notorious for this, saying things like, "Mrs. Smith you look awful." Or, "My Dad said you were a jerk." You've heard the hilarious horror stories.

As ethical adults, this is when we look back to question #1. It may be right, but will it be harmful?

Those six questions will help establish the right-or-wrong standard. Ethical questions are great for group discussions.

"Be a role model ... not a role player"

Suzy Sutton, CSP

Accountability, to stand up and be counted, to be responsible, is vital for humankind to thrive. It's our PERSONAL RESPONSIBILITY. Not the Government's ... not the Church's ... ours. Individually.

An older man, limping and bent over with a cane, has walked around the highway and side roads near my office for many years. He carries a large, plastic bag and fills it with trash. He does this faithfully. In the heat of the summer. Even on frigid winter days, there he is.

One day I stopped and thanked him for caring so much. He politely and shyly nodded, looked away and kept walking. He was doing it to make a quiet difference, not to be recognized for it.

When we are accountable, we can also take responsibility for the good that we've created in our lives. Think of all you've accomplished in the past month ... the past year ... the past decade. Good stuff doesn't just happen. You've done a lot to bring it all together.

To prove to yourself some good that you're doing, list at least 15 things you've accomplished in the past year. Mix it up with any personal, professional, social, physical, spiritual, and financial accomplishments. You'll be surprised. It's a powerful reminder.

1._____

2._____

3._____

4._____

5._____

6._____

7._____

8._____

9._____

10._____

11._____

12._____

13._____

14._____

15._____

I hope you're quite amazed. It's awesome to see accomplishments written down. The smaller ones matter, too. You're accountable for that good stuff. You've made choices that helped create it.

Now, in looking ahead ... what are some ways you can do things differently to realize your dreams, take responsibility for greater success, live more fully, and increase your happiness and contentment? Accountability counts in all areas:

PERSONAL ACCOUNTABILITY: Are you reaching your personal goals? How might you improve the quality of your family life? Do you feel good about yourself? Are you experiencing and enjoying today? Are you learning a lot?

PROFESSIONAL ACCOUNTABILITY: Is there passion in your work? Are you giving your best? How could you grow in your job? Is it fulfilling? Are you valued? Should you look into a job change?

SOCIAL ACCOUNTABILITY: Are you so overwhelmed with busy-ness that you've neglected relationships with some close, supportive friends? Do you schedule fun outings? Can they count on you?

SPIRITUAL ACCOUNTABILTY: Do you create time for matters of a higher nature? Do you sense your purpose? Is prayer or meditation part of your life? Do you look for the big picture? Do you acknowledge how greatly your actions influence others?

PHYSICAL ACCOUNTABILITY: Are you feeling well? Taking good care of yourself? Sleeping enough? Exercising? Getting regular check-ups? Eating well?

FINANCIAL ACCOUNTABILITY: How's your money situation? Are you comfortable? On the financial edge? Have low or no debt? Do you have enough for emergencies? Are you planning financially for the future?

It may seem like a lot, but when we do whatever it takes to be accountable in all areas of our lives, things run a lot smoother ... like a car running on all cylinders ... purring along. It takes plenty of "want to" and "stick to" to make it happen. The results are worth it

FORGIVENESS

It would be incomplete to talk about accountability without discussing forgiveness. And before we can truly forgive another, we must forgive ourselves for our imperfections. We are human.

Forgiveness is one of the most *difficult* actions we can take! Yet, it's one of the most powerful and empowering. It's also one of the most misunderstood concepts.

The dictionary says to "forgive" means to "pardon". I think an extension of that should be "to let go of." That means to stop harboring all that anger and negativity inside. It does NOT mean that forgiving an action discounts its seriousness. We are all accountable. And it does NOT mean that we necessarily forget the action. Instead we let go of the emotional hold it has on us.

Forgiving someone can be done directly to the source; "I forgive you for _____." Or it can be done in your heart and thoughts. You can even forgive an action done by someone who has passed on.

Forgiving is NOT justifying unacceptable behavior. It simply means, "I acknowledge the hurtful behavior. Although I don't accept it, I've decided to let go of it."

Choosing to forgive an action doesn't automatically turn one into a door mat to be stepped on by everyone. Quite the opposite ... because it was a choice.

Forgiveness is an action that takes a lot of time and readiness. If it happens too quickly I'd question the motive. Remember back as kids the grownups would hurry this process with: "Tell Patty you're sorry." Then they'd follow with, "Patty, now tell Kevin it's okay." Was that really from the heart????

Forgiving doesn't necessarily mean things are back to business as usual. You may have come to the realization that you forgive this person but no longer want to continue a relationship. Maybe you're both growing in very different directions and you feel it's time to move on.

Having a past with someone doesn't always justify having a present or future with them. Weighing it out with a professional helps in these cases. An objective third party can make a huge difference.

CHARITY

We can't end this chapter on accountability without talking about charity. Giving back to those in need ... who are facing less fortunate circumstances than we are.

Some of the happiest, most alive people I've ever met are those who give a lot. They give their time. Some give financial help. Some can give both. It's all a contribution to the greater good of human-kind. And the greatest gift is to the giver.

*Lord, make me an
instrument of Your peace.
Where there is hatred
let me sow
love;
where there is injury,
pardon;
where there is doubt,
faith;
where there is despair,
hope;
where there is darkness,
light;
And where there is sadness,
joy.*

ST. FRANCIS OF ASSISI

REVIEW

You can't lead ... where you won't go.

To keep fired up be accountable!

Do your **ACTIONS** pass the ethics test?

    1. Will it harm others or yourself?

    2. Is it fair?

    3. Does it pass the front page test?

    4. Is it honest?

    5. Do I believe in it?

    6. Is it right?

Are you **ACCOUNTABLE** ...

    Personally?

    Professionally?

    Socially?

    Spiritually?

    Physically?

    Financially?

CHAPTER EIGHT

TAKE YOUR TIME

"Positives, negatives, everywhere you look
War and peace in every history book
If you take life too seriously
You might check out prematurely

Take your time, what's your hurry?
Stop and smell the roses along the way
Take your time, there's no need to worry
Enjoy the situation ... have a wonderful day!"

Anderson/McCree

Whoa. Slow down. Come in for a landing. Unravel. In Chapter Three we covered the importance of living in the "now". Here we'll go over some specifics in learning *how* to take your time.

Taking your time means slowing down enough to have more fun. Being alive. Enjoying what's happening *today*. Lightening up.

Baseball legend Stan Musial comes to mind. I was performing at a celebrity golf tournament show in Iowa. After the program, there was an impromptu jam session in the hotel lobby. Stan pulled a harmonica out of his pocket and started playing his heart out with the other musicians. He was pretty good, too.

But most memorable was the smile on his face. What a great time he was having. It didn't matter if every note was perfect. He was in there swinging. Enjoying the situation to the max.

Our time is one of our most valuable assets. We need to treat it like a treasure.

"If you think life is a race ...
you'll just keep going
around in circles."

CGA

Will this chapter be helpful to you? Should you take the time to read it? Answer the short questionnaire below to find out:

1. It's harder to keep up with everything I need to do.

    Yes___ No___

2. Lately, it seems like I've been working more hours.

    Yes___ No___

3. It seems like time is flying by faster and faster.

    Yes___ No___

4. I envy people who have more time for fun.

    Yes___ No___

5. I'm almost always in a hurry.

    Yes___ No___

6. It's hard for me to sometimes just do nothing.

    Yes___ No___

7. I don't have time to take good care of myself.

    Yes___ No___

8. I should spend more time with my loved ones.

    Yes___ No___

So, how'd you do? If you answered "yes" to any of the above, read on. You might find some helpful hints here.

STOP, LOOK, and LISTEN

We learned that phrase in first grade. As adults, we can apply the concept to more than just crossing the street. It has a very broad and valuable application.

"Stop, Look, and Listen" is good advice for anyone starting a business, entering into a romantic relationship, buying a house, making a career change ... anything. And it's essential in getting fired up without burning out! Let's take a closer look.

STOP!

Isn't it ironic that to move forward, sometimes we've got to stop? Athletes are a prime example. They work their bodies hard. They're in good physical shape, but they have to rest their muscles between games, matches, or even work-outs. That's how they replenish their energy ... how they get fired up again. If they don't stop, they're in danger of injury ... maybe even permanent damage.

We ALL have to stop, assess, rest, re-group. When we do, we open our minds to new heights and greater creativity. Have you noticed how you often get some of your best ideas ... real problem-solvers ... when you're just about to fall asleep, or just waking up? That's the dreamy Alpha state. Novelist Saul Bellow calls this, "dream space."

Many powerful inventions, song ideas, solutions to everyday challenges, book passages, etc. come to mind in this important state of relaxation. If our minds are filled with "to do" lists, there's not much room for new ideas to flow through.

We all need to slow down and re-charge our batteries. If we try to keep going at break-neck speed, something beyond our control may come along to force us to slow down.

If we're listening, it could be a wake-up call. And it may come in a variety of ways; the loss of a job due to downsizing, a serious illness or death in the family, depression, loss of a relationship, a serious accident, on and on.

One way to avoid an outside warning is to be more in tune with what your mind and body are trying to tell you. When you stop, you make that possible.

It's not always easy to stop and pull over to the side of the fast track to re-fuel. Some even have every minute of their vacations filled with activity. But slowing down needs to be a priority!

"We've got to make the time ... to take our time."

CGA

LOOK!

Okay, so once we stop, what do we *look* for? One way to look closely is to check in with some focused questions. As the Chairperson of your life, the President and CEO of yourself, hold a news conference with *you*!

At this personalized conference ask yourself, WHO? WHAT? WHEN? WHERE? WHY? For example: "At this stage of the game, who am I, really?" List the characteristics that you feel would describe you. Include feedback you've gotten from others.

Next ask, "What do I want to get and give back in my life? Am I doing what I truly believe in? Am I using my strengths and talents?"

Then, "When do I plan to reach my short and long-term goals? Do I want to modify them? Simplify them?" Look back to Chapter One.

Next ask, "Where do I see myself next month? Next year? In five years? Do my loved ones fit into the plan?"

Finally, "Why am I making the decisions I've chosen? Am I fulfilled? Growing? Hopeful? Responsibile?"

It can be a challenge to look at yourself objectively. Do your best. Only when we look carefully and intentionally can we really see.

LISTEN!

What an art listening is. I mean to truly LISTEN one hundred percent ... not planning your answer. It takes energy to keep the mind so focused. No wonder the old wisdom is that you can't learn while you're talking.

One of my all-time favorite stories is about listening, and I tell it respectfully:

An older man was proud of his new hearing aid and was showing it off to his friends. He told them how small they can make them now and how affordable and effective they are.

Impressed with all this, a friend asked, "What kind is it?"

"Oh, about 10:30," he answered. (I love that story.)

Listening to others we respect can teach us volumes. Ask questions of those you admire who seem to be living life to the fullest, who radiate happiness and contentment, who are fired up! Most happy, successful people are willing and honored to share their knowledge.

When we sharpen our listening tool we not only learn a lot about others ... but also ourselves. The more you listen to your own inner voice, the more wisdom you'll uncover there. Lots of it.

Sometimes that little voice is trying to tell us something we don't want to hear. It may mean that to heed that information, we'll have to change something. If we're not ready, we'll ignore it. It keeps coming back, though, if we're listening. Do you hear it?

If you STOP, LOOK, and LISTEN, you'll be able to move forward in a new enlightened and inspired way.

OUR MOST VALUABLE ASSETS: H.A.L.T.

Yes, our most valuable assets ... this means all of us ... are: Health, Awareness, Love, Time. Notice they're all intangible. I put them in this order only because I think the acronym (HALT) makes the concept easy to remember.

HEALTH

You know how miserable it is to do anything when you don't feel well. Whether you just feel a little off or have a humdinger of a head cold, it's no picnic trying to plow through the day. Imagine then, having a serious illness, or one with a less-than-hopeful prognosis, or being in chronic pain. All the tea in China or all the money on the planet doesn't make it feel better. Good health matters.

AWARENESS

How tragic it is to see someone who's physically okay but whose mind is not fully functioning ... or gone completely. To be confused about very simple things once taken for granted must be very frustrating and painful. Oh what they'd give to have mental clarity again.

LOVE

Love. It's a complete sentence all by itself. In the next chapter, we'll talk a lot about this vital topic.

*"All you need
is love."*

The Beatles

TIME

Last, but by no means least of our four most valuable assets, TIME is one of those buzzwords. Think of how often we refer to it every single day. How many times have you consulted a clock or watch so far today?

Time is a measure of duration. It's also what keeps everything from happening at once. Without time, would we be here? Does time flow in a straight time-line? A circle? Can we really "waste" time or "save" time? How do you spend your time?

Keep all four of these precious assets in mind. When you "take your time" you can appreciate them all more.

DE-STRESS FOR SUCCESS

We can't go a step further without talking about the MIND/BODY connection. They're not just connected, they're intertwined. Stress is a clear example.

Have you ever had a "tension" headache? A "nervous" stomach? Ulcers? High blood pressure? Heart palpitations? Migraines? Most are stress-induced with real, physical reactions. I know someone who gets a migraine headache every Sunday evening, right before the new work week. Think it may be related to a stressful job?

Seventy-five percent of complaints made to primary physicians are stress related. Job stress costs U.S. industry more than $200 *billion* per year. A Blue-Cross/Blue-Shield report found that five out of six workers felt job stress played a major factor in their illnesses.

The wild thing is that stress exists completely in our minds! It's not based on the conditions … but once again, on our *decisions* about them. It's our perception of what's happening.

Back to the traffic analogy; being stuck in traffic may drive you bonkers and stress you out completely. The next person may love the extra quiet time from the unexpected delay.

A simple event like a birthday is another example. The excited young adult is looking forward to his/her 21st birthday. To the person who's turning 40 next week, there may be a more stressful reaction. Which shows us that we all need to change our perception on aging in general… especially since we're living more active lives longer. Another reason to take the time to enjoy it all.

Stress is not always negative. A moment of stress could be lifesaving. It's that fight or flight response we get naturally in times of real danger.

As a teenager, my family and I lived at a camp/ranch for inner-city youth. Dad was the director. Late one night, the Neversink River, which bordered the camp, flooded its banks. It was raging!

Mom carried Mary Beth, still very young, in her arms while I held on to her for dear life. We struggled to safety. My older sister, Lynn, was marooned with about sixty kids in a small cabin. A hundred or so other campers were screaming and stranded near the rushing waters.

Dad went out in the murky night to help with rescue efforts of military helicopters and firefighters. The stress gave him super strength against the powerful current ... motorboats were even capsizing. He helped bring each child to safety. All survived.

That was an example of good stress. Temporary stress. But daily, prolonged stress is a different animal altogether. We weren't built to maintain a stressful mode. It's hazardous to our health!

WHAT CAUSES STRESS?

Some stress in our lives is unavoidable. In life, comes loss. Loss of loved ones, jobs, belongings ... even our youth. Multiple losses at once are especially difficult. This is when we *must* reach out for support. Asking for help is not a sign of weakness. It's a sign of strength.

Prolonged, daily stress is a result of our thoughts about our situation. Remember, it's not the situation itself. Erroneous perceptions create it. Here's a sampling:

"I can't afford to slow down."

"I have to do it perfectly or not at all!"

"Maybe some day I can enjoy life, but not right now ... I've got too much to do."

"I feel overwhelmed and there's nothing I can do about it."

"This relationship is pretty bad, but it's better than nothing."

"I hate my job, but there's probably nothing better out there."

These statements would create stress in anybody! If you look closely, they all have an attitude of "stuckness." If we feel we have no control over our lives, we're in trouble. Victims ... not winners.

WHAT TO DO?

CHANGE YOUR THOUGHTS, for starters, to empowering ones:

"I AM." "I CAN." "I WILL."

Remember the important action of affirming back in Chapter Four. You can never affirm powerful, positive thoughts too much! Those words "I CAN" for example;

stick them all over the place. These important words will energize, empower, and help relieve stress. Our thoughts do create our actions.

LEARN TO DELEGATE. Let go of some things. You don't have to do it all. You can't. Remember the wise adage; "You're a human being, not a human doing!"

BE MORE FLEXIBLE. Two signs of real mental fitness are the ability to bounce back after a setback, and to be open-minded.

LEARN TO SAY, "SO WHAT?" about more circumstances. It's easy to get caught up in the smallest details and lose sight of the whole thing. Let go and loosen up.

SAY "NO" more often. It's an important way to de-stress. Here's more on this:

"NO" IS A WONDERFUL WORD

Lots of us grew up with the idea that saying "no" to a nice person or organization was unacceptable. "What would they think of us?" You know how difficult it can be just dealing with those unsolicited sales calls at home. And we've never even *met* those people.

"No" is one of the most important and powerful words in language. It's also one of the hardest words to say for much of the population. But it's not too late.

You can start working on this "no" thing now. It may take a little time to break the old habit. If you often say "yes" when you really want to say "no", here's some help.

These are three good tips in learning to say "no". With the P.I.P. Method, your "no" should be:

1. *POLITE* - "No, I can't, but I hope it works out for you." You're being clear yet very polite.

2. *IMMEDIATE* - Drop the "no" in right away so it's an immediate, powerful statement. Example: "No, my schedule is packed right now."

3. *PERSISTENT* - Sometimes we're not heard the first time. A friend may say, "Oh, c'mon ... sure you can ..." This is when we have to repeat our first statement, "No, I really can't ..."

You'll be so glad you said "no". And you *don't* need to give a detailed explanation of why not. This all may take some practice. Take a deep breath and try it in the car. Get used to hearing yourself say it. This could drastically improve your life!

WHY TAKE GOOD CARE OF YOURSELF?

When you take good care of yourself, *you* not only benefit, but you have much more to give ... I've flown hundreds of thousands of miles and on each commercial flight, the flight attendant gives the same message. It goes something like this:

"Please fasten your seatbelts. Notice where the exits are. In case of the loss of cabin pressure, yellow oxygen masks will automatically be lowered from overhead. Place this mask over your nose and mouth and affix it behind your ears ... until you are breathing comfortably. THEN, if you are traveling with small children, put on their oxygen masks and see that *they* are breathing comfortably."

This is a strong metaphor for life. Unless we take care of *ourselves*, we can't truly take care of others. We won't have the strength. We'll run out of steam. Again, it's not selfish. It's SELF CARE.

Picture a glass of water. Imagine that all the time, love, and energy you have is represented by that water. Then think of how quickly that water can drain out of there ... being used up by priority needs; family, work, home chores, etc. After that may come those things we agreed to and now regret. If we didn't schedule time in for ourselves, we'll be lost in the shuffle ... running on empty. That can't last long.

"For different results ...
do something different!"

Unknown

The key to changing things is to START *NOW*. START *SMALL*. Break big things down into smaller pieces and they become much easier.

My sister Lynn and her husband Jerry find that creating a beautiful garden is a great way to "take their time" in their busy lives. And the results are fragrant and gorgeous. Find out what works for you ... then go ahead and do it.

In the early 1900s, Sibyl F. Partridge came up with a daily plan that I feel summarizes the essence of this chapter:

JUST FOR TODAY

Just for today I will be happy.

Just for today I will try to adjust myself to what is, and not try to change anyone or anything. I will take my family, my business, and my luck just as they come.

Just for today I will take care of my body. I will exercise it, nourish it, and not abuse it with drugs or alcohol.

Just for today I will improve my mind by learning something useful. I will read something that requires concentration.

Just for today I will do a good deed for someone.

Just for today I will be agreeable, courteous and liberal with praise.

Just for today I will write down my goals and plans ... I will eliminate hurry and indecision.

Just for today I will have a quiet half hour all by myself to relax and think of God.

Just for today I will be unafraid to enjoy what is beautiful. I will love and believe that those I love, love me.

Just for today I will live just this day, today.

REVIEW

TAKE YOUR TIME ... to get fired up without burning out!

STOP - Come in for a landing. Take a break.

LOOK - Get a clear idea of your life.

LISTEN - Hear that inner voice. Your gut instinct.

Assess your most valuable assets:

HEALTH
AWARENESS
LOVE
TIME

De-stress for success:

Change your thoughts
Learn to delegate
Be more flexible
Say "so what?" more often
Say "no" more often

CHAPTER NINE

LOVE MATTERS MOST

"Life is a journey with so many turns
So many lessons not easy to learn
When we look into each other's eyes
We find the secret that helps us get by.

Love matters most
We can keep looking
But nothing comes close
When we get to the end of the line
We'll find ...
Love matters most

In the dark of night
It seems like nobody's home
The love is in your heart
You're never alone."

Anderson/McCree

Books, poems, greeting cards, movies, songs, letters, phone calls ... there's lots about love. All types of love. Yet, we've had a tough time trying to adequately define it for years.

Love. We've been trying to get into it, wondering how to stay in it, dealing with being out of it, realizing there are many different levels of it ... since the beginning.

Love is here or it's gone. Love is right or it's wrong. Love can be a little or a lot. It's clear or confusing. Or both. One thing for certain, it's important.

We can love another person, our family members, our dog, our computer, spaghetti, our job, the sunset, a long nap, jelly beans, sports, painting, a '57 Chevy, folded laundry, a Texas two-step, money, the city, the country ... you name it.

The dictionary isn't much help here. It says that "love" is "a strong feeling of affection for someone or something." That sounds a little too simple. But maybe that's all we need to know.

Love is a feeling that's intangible and hard to measure. It's also hard to explain ... premature babies who get massaged by nurses gain up to 47% more weight than premature babies who don't. That's a powerful statistic.

Other recent studies found that when we experience the affection of having a pet, our blood pressure actually lowers from the calming effect. Other studies show that when we maintain close ties with other people, we enjoy better overall health. LOVE IS HEALTHY.

> *"On their deathbed ... no-one says*
> *'I wish I'd have spent*
> *more time at the office ...*
> *or cleaning house.'"*
>
> **Unknown**

Rather, they may wish they'd have spent more quality time with their loved ones. Telling them how much they mattered. Here's a story that drives this point home:

A LOVE STORY

Roy Clark has been traveling around the world performing since he was seventeen. Through the years, he always looked forward to going back to visit his folks whenever he had some time off. When he'd walk through the door, he'd give his Mama a big hug and tell her he loved her. He'd automatically stick his hand out for a hearty hand-shake with his Dad.

This routine went on for years. As his career progressed, the demands became greater and visits to his folks became rarer and even more special. He decided to try something different.

On his next visit home, he gave his Mom a big hug and told her he loved her, as usual. But instead of the predictable handshake with his Dad, he pushed his hand away. He gave him a big hug and told his Dad he loved him too!

Hester Clark was speechless ... and pretty uncomfortable. He didn't know what to make of this. They had never hugged as adults and just always assumed they loved each other. But over time, this became a new pattern and less awkward.

Now here's the kicker: A few years into this new routine, Roy and his wife, exhausted from traveling, arrived at his folks' home for Christmas. As usual, Roy gave his Mama a big hug and told her he loved her. For some reason, he wasn't thinking and reached out to shake his Dad's hand.

His Dad, now happy with the new routine, pushed Roy's hand away and gave him a great, big hug and said how much he loved him!

Roy Clark's parents have both sinced passed away. Is he ever glad he took those precious opportunities to share his loving feelings with them.

A LOVE SONG

Love is way too valuable to be taken for granted. We can never say "I love you" *too* many times. We can't hear it too much either.

My friend Debbie Hupp came up with a novel way to tell her kids how much she loved them. Along with telling them over and over, she wrote her feelings in a song. You've probably heard it. The title is, "YOU DECORATED MY LIFE". Kenny Rogers heard it, fell in love with it, and recorded it. The song became a huge pop and country hit. It also won Debbie a well-deserved Grammy for "song of the year."

If I were asked to summarize the message of the Bible, I would quote the following two verses:

"Beloved, let us love one another:
for love is of God;
and every one that loveth
is born of God, and knoweth God.
He that loveth not
knoweth not God;
for God is love."

I John 4:7 & 8

Is there plenty of love in your life? The need to love and be loved is part of being human. If you're not surrounded by a loving family, create one ... choose to be with friends who are mutually loving and supportive. Make it a point to get together regularly. Build a solid relationship. There's an abundance of love to go around ... we just have to make the space for it.

We can't get fired up without burning out unless we have some love in our lives. No one is an island ... we don't have to stand alone. We *need* each other.

FOR LOVE OR MONEY?

Can money replace love? Several follow-up studies have been done with lottery winners. The results are interesting; After two years, many winners said the financial windfall was more of a hassle than a help. At first, they had lots of fun paying off debts and buying new things. The problems came when their priorities changed, when they were pressured with how to spend it, etc.

Some said that after giving up their jobs, they started missing feeling productive and relating to co-workers. Others said it even ended their marriages. Often the reaction was, "We were happier when we were struggling to make ends meet ... life was simpler." It's too bad money can't buy true love.

SO, WHERE'S THE LOVE?

Because of the great value of love, there are many issues around it. Many find it difficult to give or receive love comfortably. Experiencing a loss of love in childhood can have long-range results. Even the perception of the loss has consequences. The self-help sections of bookstores and libraries are loaded with books dealing with the love struggle.

Many experts agree that the degree to which we can love others is directly related to the degree we love ourselves. Once again, the Bible has a good tip on this: "Love thy neighbor as *thyself*."

It's NOT a sign of narcissism or self-centeredness to love oneself ... if we love others too. In fact, this is what self-esteem is based on ... treating ourselves with love and respect.

Unfortunately, many years ago an erroneous message got out that to love oneself was thoughtless and selfish. That we should only focus on the needs of others. Everyone else was more important.

Then part of society swung the other way into the "ME" decade. We don't want to retrace those steps by any means either.

The good news is that we can turn this around ... slowly but surely. It's never too late to learn to love yourself. The results are worth the effort. This has an impact on every aspect of our lives.

A LOVE PLAN THAT WORKS

Since greater self-love and respect can be learned at any age, here are some specifics:

SELF-APPROVAL - To really love oneself, you must let go of any negative opinions about yourself that are yours or others.   This does not mean you assume that you are perfect! Who in the world could live up to that? It means that you are working on *improving* the wonderful you all the time ... BUT YOU APPROVE OF YOU NOW. It doesn't mean that you accept no responsibility for your actions. But that you approve of you as a person.

Just as we discussed in Chapter Four, we've also got to affirm self-approval. Get used to saying, "I approve of myself" and "I like myself" all day long. Make it a habit. Remember, what we focus on becomes our reality.

No matter what you want to change about you ... let's say you want to lose weight, set better boundaries, stop smoking, stop spending, get a more challenging job, whatever it is ... acknowledge those things you will be changing and still approve of you now.

"You are not perfect ...
you are a lovable human being
under construction."

CGA

Here again is why it's so vital to spend more time with positive, supportive people. If you hear lots of negative messages, that's what your subconscious believes. It takes a lot of work to overpower it with the good, positive stuff. But you can start now.

SELF-ASSESSMENT - Another important way toward self-love and confidence is self-assessment. Get a handle on your positive traits. Most people have focused on the negative, ignoring anything positive. Write down all your good traits that you can think of. Since it's difficult to be objective, it would also be helpful to ask some close friends or family members to describe you.

You can begin here. SOME OF MY GREAT TRAITS ARE:

_____   _____

_____   _____

_____   _____

_____   _____

_____   _____

Keep adding to the list and include all compliments you can remember. List all new ones. Look back to this and the above lists a lot! When you need a boost, there it is ... in all its beautiful glory.

SELF-SUPPORT - Now that you're getting better acquainted with self-approval and self-assessment, you can go forward with self-support. Start thinking in terms of:

"I deserve more time with my family, so I will:

_____."

"I deserve better health, so I will:

_____."

"I deserve a loving relationship, therefore I will:

_____."

"I deserve greater financial security, so I will:

_____."

Notice that building better self-love includes taking full responsibility for our choices. That powerfully adds to our self-love and respect.

> *"Remember, no one can make*
> *you feel inferior*
> *without your consent."*
>
> **Eleanor Roosevelt**

STAND UP AND BREATHE - When walking, standing, or even sitting, stay as straight as you comfortably can. This adds a lot to your confidence level. Also, breathe more deeply. That also helps to relieve anxiety and raise confidence. Practice it right now and you'll see how effective it is.

SEND LOVE MESSAGES - To you! I have a friend who sometimes calls her answering machine from work and leaves herself a sweet, loving message. When she gets home from an especially hard day, she hears that ray of sunshine. See what works for you.

TREAT YOURSELF LOVINGLY - As though you were a treasured object. You *are*. Be easy on yourself. Take good care of yourself. Notice the good things you do through the day and give yourself a pat on the back. Treat yourself by celebrating even your smallest accomplishments. Have fun with it.

Follow the above LOVE PLAN and you'll see your self-love, self-esteem, self-respect and confidence ... take giant steps forward.

"BUT, I DON'T HAVE TIME FOR MYSELF"

How can we raise our level of self-love and respect ... and avoid burning out ... if we don't give ourselves any time? We can't! We've *got* to carve out the time. If you believe you're worth even 1% of your time, here's the no-excuse way to do it.

Find a quiet place and commit to this simple pattern:

Anderson's **"TRIPLE 7"** Survival Plan

7 MINUTES EVERY MORNING:

Praise yourself for any improvements you're making.
Plan your day in your mind.
Picture the successful outcome of your goals.

7 MINUTES EVERY EVENING:

Praise yourself for the good things you did today.
Plan your day out for tomorrow.
Picture everything working out smoothly.

7 DAYS A WEEK:

Make this a part of your daily ritual. It can have far-reaching results. Do it for 21 days and assess the amazing benefits.

There are 1,440 minutes in each full day. If you follow this plan, you are giving yourself 14 minutes. That's less than 1% of the entire day. Such a deal! You sure are worth it. Big time.

THE MORE LOVE YOU HAVE ...
THE MORE YOU CAN GIVE

As we give ourselves more time, approval, and love ... a magical thing happens; we have much more to give away. And the more we give away, the more we get back. What a great, full circle of love!

There's no more wonderful, complete feeling than loving and being loved.

"Spread love everywhere you go; first of all in your own house. Give love to your children, to your wife or husband, to a next door neighbor ... Let no one ever come to you without leaving better and happier. Be the living expression of God's kindness; kindness in your face, kindness in your eyes, kindness in your smile, kindness in your warm greeting."

Mother Teresa

LOVE YOUR WORK

Once again, we can't have a life full of love if we don't love what we do. Whether you have a job, a career, are a full-time parent, or even retired, make it a point to love and enjoy your daily chores. Find a way. Try new, refreshing ways of looking at things.

A couple of weeks ago, I gave a presentation in New Jersey. After the program, a big, burly gentleman came up to say hello and showed me something he was real proud of. He was holding a box with a magnificent bird on a twig inside.

"Is that real or stuffed?" I asked in amazement.

"Neither", he answered. "I carved it out of a piece of wood. And I'd like you to have it as a gift," he said ... a little choked up.

Pete was a retired transmission mechanic. Recently recovering from quadruple by-pass heart surgery, he spent countless hours carving gorgeous pieces like the beautiful bird. His rough, worn hands now create delicate objects ... and he loves doing it!

LIFE CAN BE A CIRCUS

And speaking of loving your work, I have clear memories of some of our neighbors back in that little trailer park I told you about. Many of them were circus performers with the Big Top Circus televised from New York City.

I remember walking down the narrow rows of trailers and seeing incredible things; the performers practicing their acts over and over again. A pair of teenage twins, Barbara and Betty, would be walking a tightrope *and* doing flips. Their brother would watch for any slips.

Further down the lane, an older man with his Chihuahua on his shoulder, would climb a tall, narrow, shiny ladder that was not leaning against anything! Balance with a capital "B".

Next were the Brewsters. This couple roller-skated in fast circles on a small, portable, wooden platform they set up on their tiny patio. The husband would spin the wife so fast, her body was horizontal.

All these performers looked like they were having a ball ... even during those long practices.

You might feel as though *you* are sometimes walking a tightrope, doing a balancing act, or spinning in circles on *your* job. The trick is to find something you enjoy about it. Make it interesting. Your attitude makes a powerful difference.

And to repeat an important point; if you strongly dislike your job and have sincerely tried to turn things around ... take responsibility for putting your gifted energy, time and interest into something else. A big step with big results. When we're more fulfilled it reflects on those around us. Everyone benefits.

LOVING STUFF TO DO

You've heard people say, "We used to have so much fun, but now there's not that much to do." "We can't afford to go out anymore." "By the end of the day, there's no time left for us." "There aren't a lot of nice things to do for yourself if you're single."

Whether you're single, dating, married, financially challenged (nearly broke), or financially secure ... there's something here for you. Check out this list of suggestions:

* Light candles at dinner ... even at Sunday breakfast.

* Buy a tin kazoo and learn to play it. (It's fun and easy.)

* Fly a kite.

* Watch some old Marx Brothers movies.

* Visit the local zoo. (Not necessarily your neighbor's house.)

* Go to a high school football game. Enjoy the memories.

* Plan a miniature golf party.

* Put on a '50s tape and dance your heart out. No partner necessary.

* Have a bowling night out.

* Visit a local attraction you thought was way too touristy.

* Produce a short mystery movie with your video camera.

* Create a great new Chili recipe.

* Go to a free, local concert. Sing all the way home.

* Take a sculpture class ... with friends or meet new ones.

* Spend the day at a big flea market. Talk with the vendors.

* Throw an old-fashioned 4th of July party.

* Go for a walk in the rain ... hit every puddle!

* Sit by a fire and sip hot chocolate.

* Watch *Bambi* and *Fantasia* again.

* Plan a campout with a bunch of friends ... even in the back yard.

* Go visit pawn shops.

* Get into some beautiful chamber music.

* Have breakfast at a local truckstop.

* Take a long, relaxing bath ... with candles. Sip a special beverage.

* Pick wildflowers in a field.

* Have a Pictionary party. Laugh yourself silly.

* Park near an airport and watch the airplanes. Imagine the
  possibilities.

* Go to the State Fair. See everything.

* Drop in on your town's night court ... it's another world.

* Volunteer at a Children's Hospital or Nursing Home.

* Get a book of easy magic tricks ... amaze your friends.

* Take a short train ride out of town.

* Visit your local art gallery. Expand your vision.

* Hug ... every chance you get.

* Add a bunch of your own. Love it up!

REVIEW

LOVE MATTERS MOST and keeps you fired up.

Learn to love yourself ... here's how:

    Self-approval
    Self-assessment
    Self-support
    Stand up and breathe deeply
    Send love messages
    Treat yourself lovingly

Anderson's "TRIPLE 7" Survival Plan

Give yourself 14 minutes a day. Break it down like this:

    7 minutes every morning
    7 minutes every evening
    7 days a week

More love points:

The more love you give ... the more love you receive

Review the 35 fun suggestions

CHAPTER TEN

FLYING

---

*"Aerodynamically, the bumble bee
shouldn't be able to fly,
but the bumble bee
doesn't know it
so it goes on flying anyway."*

Mary Kay Ash

I like feathers. It could be that they represent wings. And wings represent flying ... which is neat.

Soon after sister Mary Beth flew off to the next life, I looked up in the sky and saw a huge, detailed feather formed out of a cloud. The warm chill I got from gazing up at it told me she was sending a soft, real message that all was well. I keep finding feathers.

One of my early childhood memories was going to a small airport with my Dad and older sister Lynn. Sometimes we'd get a Dairy Queen before we watched all those planes landing and taking off. There was something very fascinating and magical about flying.

SEEING THE BIG PICTURE

My Dad, 81, still has a valid, current pilot's license and flies with friends every week. He likes the view from high above. A different perspective.

A neighbor always seemed very predictable to me. She'd put up decorations for each holiday on the same day every year. She'd schedule family vacations at least a year in advance, plan her menus a week ahead, etc. A Martha Stewart dream.

One day I asked her husband where Fran was ... I hadn't been seeing her around much. "Fran is flying," he answered.

"Oh, is she off on business? A family visit?" I casually asked.

"No, Fran's flying ... flying a plane! She wanted to do something adventurous, so she got her pilot's license. She can't get enough of it. In fact, Fran often circles our neighborhood and says it looks great from the air." (Fran now also skydives *and* has a tattoo).

Wow, was I caught red-handed in the prejudging department.

A friend has a beautiful garden surrounding his home. Paul enjoys all the hard work it takes ... good exercise after the office. He tries his best to keep it weed-free, which is no easy task.

After a recent storm, Paul went up on his roof to remove a fallen branch. While he was way up there, he looked down at his garden. It looked picture perfect. From that vantage point ... immaculate.

The big picture is an important viewpoint. There, we don't notice the petty, little, mundane things that don't amount to diddly in the long run. Focus on the big picture more.

ARE YOU SOARING LIKE AN EAGLE?

To keep fired up without burning out, you've got to fly! Are you flying? Are you moving through life as though you sometimes had wings? Sailing through the air?

THE POTENTIAL PYRAMID

To find out if you're flying, living near your powerful potential, I'd like you to see where you fit in this potential pyramid:

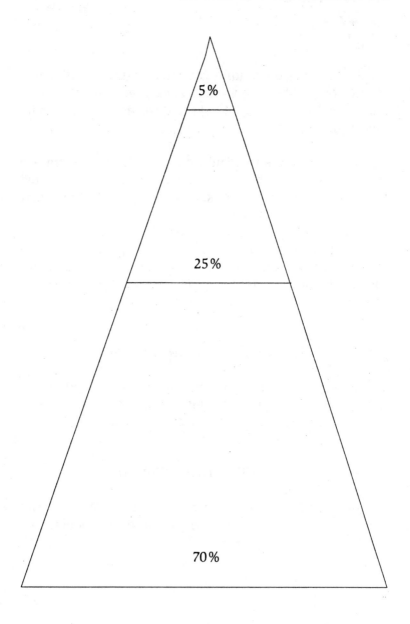

THE 70% GROUP: At the bottom is the widest section of this triangle shape. I'd say approximately 70% of the population is at this low end ... far from reaching their potential. Sadly, that's a lot of people.

The characteristics of this lower level are:

Existing in a hum-drum pattern of life.

Living in the past or future rather than in this moment.

Not feeling much of anything ... pain or pleasure.

Knowing there could be much more, but taking no action.

Not learning and growing. Just getting by.

Feeling somewhat defeated ... "What's the use?"

No clear goals, plans, or focus.

Rushing through each day.

THE 25% GROUP: In the mid-section of the pyramid of potential, are about 25% of the population who give it a shot. These folks experience some glimpses of being fired up but, unfortunately, don't stay there.

Some characteristics of this middle group are:

Taking healthy risks only *now and then.*

Don't *always* fear failure and rejection.

Create *occasional* balance in their lives.

Learn from *some* mistakes.

Occasionally enjoy simple beauty.

Only *intermittently* growing as a person.

THE 5% GROUP: This is the top of the mountain. About 5% of the population is among this elite bunch. These folks are very close to their potential ... to, as the Army says, "Being all that you can be."

A few characteristics of this high level are:

Set and reach many goals.

Maintain balance. Priorities are *always* considered.

Think of better solutions to everyday problems.

Savor every moment.

Growing and learning every day.

Enjoy giving as much as receiving.

Love to take healthy risks. Don't fear failure.

Value all kinds of ideas and beliefs.

STARTING AT THE TOP!

Where do *you* stand on this scale? If you're not at the top, why not? After all, YOU STARTED AT THE TOP! Think about it; when we come into the world, we're a blank slate ready to be imprinted with whatever our surroundings have to give.

We're born with only two fears according to behavioral experts. Fear of falling and fear of loud noise. All other fears are learned. Not reaching our potential has a lot to do with fear of failure and other learned fears.

A baby is completely open to new ideas ... even thrives on them. Babies savor every moment, have no prejudice, feel all their feelings, are fully alive ... fully present ... and they sure let us know about it.

SO, WHAT HAPPENED?

It's the socialization process. It starts with whatever we're surrounded with; our families, TV, school, peers, magazines, etc. Sometimes we get a message that "if we're not like everyone else, we're not valuable or even acceptable."

Remember back to the wild Christmas frenzy of "TICKLE ME ELMO" and the "BEANIE BABIES"? Kids and parents alike thought they wouldn't survive if they didn't find one of those dolls. Black-market prices shot up astronomically. The desperation was scary.

Kids think they have to wear specific brands of shoes, clothes, and hair styles, watch certain programs, eat certain foods, etc. All because they've learned that this is what they "need."

When we start school, the process really gets cranked up. In fact, to accommodate the masses, students are often given "standardized" tests. Imagine if we changed our focus from "standard" to "outstanding"? No wonder Einstein, Edison and others were thought to have learning disorders. They were extraordinary!

"Creative activity could be described
as a type of learning process
where teacher and pupil
are located
in the same individual."

Arthur Koestler

I've always found it fascinating that major softdrink companies like Pepsi and Coke have taught our society that we "need" to drink 12-ounce cans of a cold, sugary, cola mixture on a regular basis. Now it's a billion dollar industry! And it's worldwide!

TRACE, ERASE, REPLACE

The early messages we got have a profound effect. "You can do it!" or "Can't you do anything right?" both can have powerful consequences. Remember, the subconscious believes anything … true or false. So, the more we build each other up, the more empowerment we're contributing to the greater good.

Chances are that some old, negative messages* are holding you back from the top of the POTENTIAL PYRAMID. How to move forward? Trace, erase, and replace them. Think back to how they must have gotten there; they weren't helpful or intentional. Erase them … let go of the need to keep believing those messages. Replace them with much better, valid, positive stuff. Look back to the section on "AFFIRMATION" in Chapter Four.

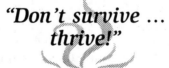

*"Don't survive …
thrive!"*

CGA

LEARNING TO FLY

To get fired up without burning out … and move up your POTENTIAL PYRAMID … you've got to fly to greater heights. Change the behaviors that are not getting you where you want to go.

GET A THOROUGH MEDICAL CHECK UP - It can't hurt to get a good once-over by an expert. Any red flags, tended to early, usually have a better prognosis.

GET A MENTAL TUNE-UP - There are now more short-term therapies available. Check in with one of these therapists for an evaluation. This can reinforce that you're on the right track. Often simple depression is discovered this way. It can be difficult to recognize ... yet it is *one of the most common and treatable* conditions.

DEAL WITH ADDICTIONS - Those recurring behaviors that have a negative impact on your family, your health, your job, your finances, or your beliefs. Knowing this, or denying the reality, you do them anyway. That's addiction and it can involve too much of anything ... worry, working, spending, sex, nicotine, sports, alcohol, eating, sleeping, gambling, drugs, computers, you name it. Addictions hold you back. Commit to overpowering them. Here again, begin by seeking the help and support of a professional and a free 12-STEP program. Both have a good track record. See what works for you.

FIND A MENTOR - We don't have to go it alone on our journey to success. A mentor is someone who has accomplished something we're striving toward. We can learn a bunch from their example. Usually they're willing and honored to help.

ACKNOWLEDGE YOUR PAIN - Pain is one of the most powerful motivators there are. If you touch a hot stove, aren't you instantly motivated to do something different? Until we acknowledge any pain from conditions we're choosing in our lives, the pain won't help us move forward.

When we do, great changes can happen. These changes may seem as painful at first, but the results make it worthwhile. You'll wonder how you stayed stuck so long.

ACKNOWLEDGE YOUR SUCCESS - Success is another great motivator. Any small taste of success can give you the drive to obtain it again. Notice each success in your life ... large and small. Let it get reinforced in your mind. Embrace the success concept. Let success fill your life in every area!

---

*Babe Ruth struck out 1,330 times ...
but he also hit 714 home runs!*

GET READY FOR TAKEOFF

Here's what you need: I call it "THE 3 W's."

1. WANTING - To take off and fly high, you have to really *want* it. To strenghten your "want to," keep focused on your goal. Realize that your dreams can truly become realities. You're the *only* one standing in your way. You deserve great things in your life. Fill it with positive input ... people and ideas. Read biographies of successful people who hung in there because they had that fire, hope, desire ... it could light a spark in you.

2. WORKING - Reaching new heights takes work. No question about that. Very successful people, inventors, leaders of all kinds, will acknowledge the amount of work ... real effort ... it took to get there. It's no accident that strenuous exercise is called "working out."

I had the pleasure of meeting the great Ray Charles. He makes a good living by singing the blues. It almost seems that international success came smooth and easy for him. But what a long, rough road he traveled to get there. Ray worked incredibly hard for many years, not to sing (that came naturally), but to hit the high note of success.

---

*"The harder you work ...
the luckier you get!"*

Various

---

3. WILLING TO PERSEVERE - Not just *wanting* and *working* make up the magic formula, but being *willing* to stay in the game during the hard times. This is the bottom line ... where the rubber meets the road. The moment of truth. There are lots of *very* talented individuals, loaded with potential, who haven't chosen to persevere. That is all that separates them from reaching great heights.

IF I HAD MY LIFE TO LIVE OVER

I'd dare to make more mistakes next time.
I'd relax. I would limber up.
I would be sillier than I have on this trip.
I would take fewer things seriously.
I would take more chances.
I would take more trips.
I would climb more mountains and swim more rivers.
I would eat more ice cream and less beans.
I would perhaps have more actual troubles but
I'd have fewer imaginary ones.
You see, I'm one of those people who live sensibly
and sanely hour after hour, day after day.
Oh, I've had my moments and if I had it to do over
again, I'd have more of them. In fact I'd try to have
nothing else. Just moments.
One after another, instead of living so many years
ahead of each day.
I've been one of those people who never go anywhere
without a thermometer, a hot water bottle,
a raincoat and a parachute.
If I had it to do again, I would travel lighter next time.
If I had my life to live over, I would start barefoot
earlier in the spring and
stay that way later in the fall.
I would go to more dances.
I would ride more merry-go-rounds.
I would pick more daisies.

Nadine Stair wrote this at age 85

I wanted to add that wonderful poem as a reminder to
live now. Get fired up about today. Findings show that
toward the end of one's life, any regrets are not about what
we *did* ... but what we *didn't* do.

UP, UP AND AWAY!

As you prepare to fire up the engines and go zooming
down the runway toward the open sky, here are some
quick, important reminders for a smooth, fabulous flight:

"I am only one; But still I am one.
I cannot do everything,
but still I can do something;
I will not refuse to do the
something I can do."

Helen Keller

TEN TIPS FOR A *FIRED UP* LIFE!

1. BE YOURSELF. No matter how imperfect you might feel, you are the very best *you* there is. One of the greatest gifts we can give ourselves and others is to be our open, authentic selves. Let go of trying to be what you feel you "should" be. You're making progress but you are a lovable, unique creation already. By the same token, let others be who they are. You can change no one but yourself.

2. FEEL GRATEFUL. Some of my favorite behavioral experts say that if you become more mindful of all that you are grateful for, your life is forever changed. They suggest keeping a "Grateful Journal"; writing down 5 things every single day that you're grateful for. When you add that up, it comes out to 150 things a month. What positive thoughts to focus on! A sure attitude booster.

3. SIMPLIFY EVERYTHING. Get rid of the clutter in your mind, your home, your car, your office, everywhere! Be more discerning about where you put your precious energy ... including relationships. You'll create space for fresh, new energizing things to come into your life.

4. BE POSITIVE. Get in the habit of looking at the glass as half *full*. Remember, it's not the conditions we face, but our *decisions* about them. Decide to be hopeful and upbeat. A great attitude is free and available to everyone. Make that positive choice.

5. HAVE FUN. In a busy, sometimes hectic world, it's easy to lose sight of the things that really matter. "Don't sweat the small stuff" is valuable information. Make time in your schedule for fun, light things with your loved ones. Get and stay balanced.

"Start where you are.
Use what you have.
Do what you can."

Arthur Ashe

---

6. TAKE RESPONSIBILITY. Can you imagine the incredible world we'd live in if everyone took responsibility for their behavior? As soon as we blame anyone or anything for our actions, we wash our hands of responsibility. If we feel that someone or something is keeping us from greatness, we're destined to stay right where we are. Stuck in the mud. Instead, take charge of your life!

7. BELIEVE. Many experts find that belief in a Higher Power and a sense of purpose has a tremendous effect on our well-being. In fact, a recent scientific study showed that a great percentage of heart patients who were prayed for healed faster and had fewer complications. Even when they didn't know about the prayer.

8. STAY FOCUSED. Keep your eyes on the prize. Don't ever give up. Persistence is the key to positive change. That's what separates success from failure. A little at a time, done regularly, brings large results. You can do it. Hang in there. You deserve good things.

9. GIVE. Whether you give used furniture, clothing, cash, food, friendship, time, ideas, love, anything ... that gift is making a difference in the whole scheme of things. Giving is the greatest gift of all. Give all you can.

10. LIVE! Let go. Don't be afraid to fail. That will keep you from *really* living. Kick up your heels. Light the candles. Use the good dishes. Call your friends. Laugh. Cry. Love. Sing. Skip. Grow. Dance. Take the afternoon off. Enjoy this very moment. Be alive.

You've got all the tools you need to get fired up without burning out. You're worth it. Go get 'em, kiddo. Soar. Fly high!

"Turn SHOULDA, WOULDA, COULDA into....
here I go!"

CGA

REVIEW

To get fired up without burning out ... fly to new heights!

The **POTENTIAL PYRAMID:**

> Are you moving UP?

Your flight plan:

> Get a medical check up
> Get a mental tune up
> Deal with addictions
> Find a mentor
> Acknowledge your pain
> Acknowledge your success

Get ready for takeoff ... The 3 W's:

> Wanting
> Working
> Willing to persevere

Ten Tips for a *FIRED UP* Life:

> 1. Be yourself
> 2. Feel grateful
> 3. Simplify everything
> 4. Be positive
> 5. Have fun
> 6. Take responsibility
> 7. Believe
> 8. Stay focused
> 9. Give
> 10. Live!

ABOUT THE AUTHOR

Carol Grace Anderson, M.A., knows first-hand how to GET FIRED UP WITHOUT BURNING OUT! From a tiny 18' trailer, her dreams were big as the sky. carol Grace is still making those dreams come true ... she's flown with The Blue Angels, appeared on THE TONIGHT SHOW, earned a Master's Degree from New York University, toured with ROY CLARK, had two books published, had a role in the Paramount film THE THING CALLED LOVE, had over 25 of her songs recorded, performed in Russia, has a syndicated radio program ... and she's still dreaming and doing.

There have been incredible struggles along the way ... from going permanently blind in her left eye, facing tremendous financial challenges, surviving raging flood waters, and most recently, losing her younger sister way too early. But Carol Grace has learned how to turn struggle into strength and roadblocks into pathways. This books paves the way for you.

She also shares her solutions in speaking engagements across the country. From FedEx to the American Heart Association, Carol Grace has inspired thousands with her life-changing message.

For information on
Speaking Engagements:

www.getfiredup.com
or call
Anderson Programs, Inc.
800-758-2964

**More Fired Up Resources by
Carol Grace Anderson**

Get Fired Up! 10-song CD $10
A collection of 10 upbeat original songs with lyrics that inspire, empower, and motivate!

Some Angels Have Four Paws $14.95
Life lessons from our dogs. A touching, hardcover gift book that reminds us that our pets are true treasures.

The Butterfly Factor $19.95
A powerful, inspiring fable reminds teens and adults about changes, challenges, and choices in life. Includes a CD of original special music. Hardcover. Makes a great gift!

Get Fired Up! – Direct Selling Survival Guide $9.95
If you are in sales, this book teaches you the seven secrets of sales success at any level.

I Need A Good Laugh $14.95
A collection of 137 of the world's funniest quotes. You'll enjoy sharing it with your friends, family, and co-workers.